Kent Rush

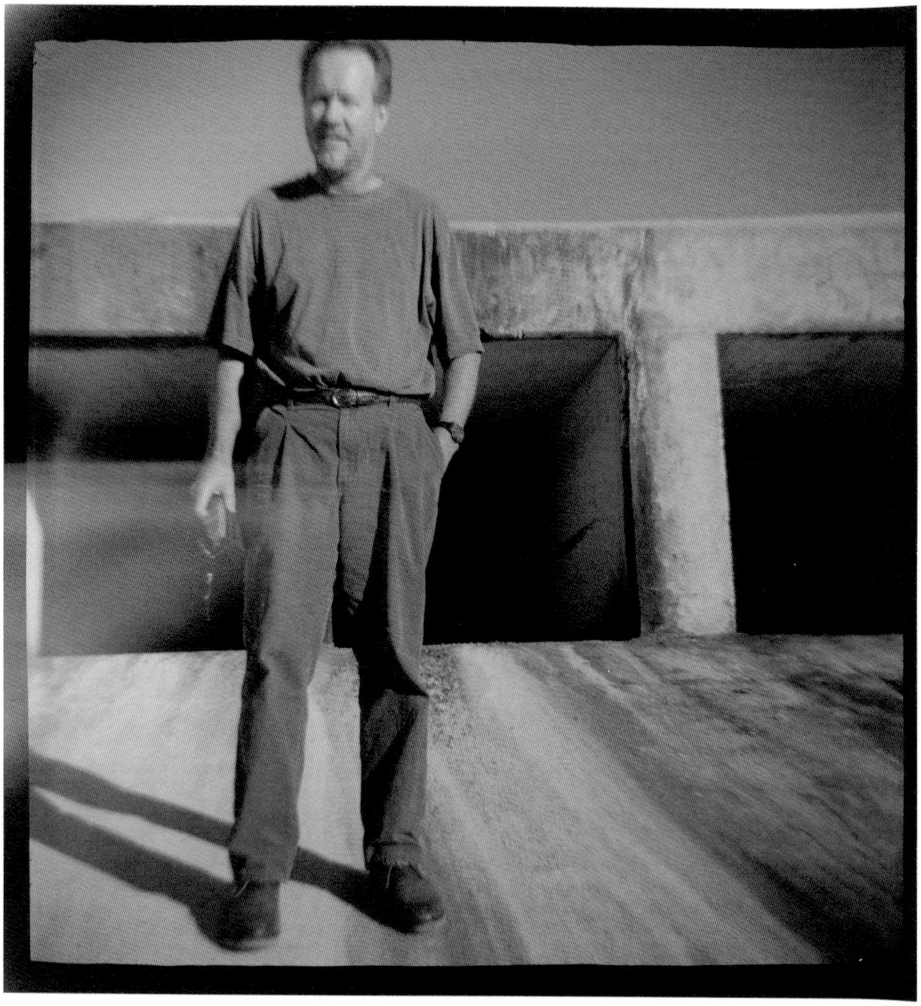

Kent Rush

A Retrospective
1970 - 1998

Lyle W. Williams

TheMcNay
The Marion Koogler McNay Art Museum

Funding for this exhibition and catalogue has been provided by Barbara and Harold Wood.

KENT RUSH:
A RETROSPECTIVE, 1970-1998
An exhibition presented at
The Marion Koogler McNay Art Museum,
San Antonio, Texas,
July 7 - August 30, 1998

Table of Contents

7 FOREWORD
William J. Chiego

8 KENT RUSH: AN APPRECIATION
Garo Z. Antreasian

10 INTRODUCTION AND ACKNOWLEDGEMENTS
Lyle W. Williams

12 KENT RUSH: LIFE AND WORK
Lyle W. Williams

30 LENDERS TO THE EXHIBITION

31 CHECKLIST

37 COLORPLATES

82 CHRONOLOGY

84 PRIVATE AND PUBLIC COLLECTIONS

88 SELECTED EXHIBITIONS

94 BIBLIOGRAPHY

96 GLOSSARY

98 PHOTO CREDITS AND COLOPHON

Foreword

In 1996, the McNay commenced a series of five retrospective exhibitions devoted to artists from San Antonio and South Texas who have made major contributions to the visual arts of our region. This series was launched because we felt it important for people to experience the long view, understanding how an artist develops over time. We firmly believe no other exhibition format can successfully accomplish the goal of examining and documenting the careers of major artists in our midst.

From the beginning, we have received support for this endeavor from Barbara and Harold Wood, who immediately understood this need and generously backed the concept with an extraordinary five-year commitment as lead sponsors. Thanks to their devotion to the artists of our community, the McNay has been able to develop such retrospective projects with a firm base of funding and provide the resources necessary to organize each exhibition and publish accompanying catalogues.

Although a departure from the McNay's past exhibition programs, the retrospective series continues a tradition established by Marion Koogler McNay. Mrs. McNay had an abiding interest in a wide range of contemporary art, including regional as well as national and international artists in her collecting scope.

This third retrospective exhibition, devoted to Kent Rush, traces and documents the career of an artist who employs a very different range of media and techniques from the two artists with whom the series began. While Reginald Rowe and Carl Rice Embrey are painters first and foremost, Kent Rush works in a variety of media, including painting, drawing, printmaking and photography. Thus it is particularly fortunate that Lyle Williams, the McNay's curator of prints and drawings, is the organizer of this exhibition and the author of its catalogue. He brings true sensitivity and insight to this rich yet subtle body of work.

We hope this exhibition and publication, like the two that preceded it, will make a lasting contribution to our understanding and appreciation of the artist's work. We also hope it will help build a permanent and growing body of knowledge of the artists in our community that will continue to grow in the coming years.

William J. Chiego, Director

Kent Rush: An Appreciation

I am so pleased that the McNay Art Museum is mounting this retrospective exhibition of Kent Rush at the mid-point of an outstanding and productive career. I am confident that it will reconfirm the stature of Kent's art for those already familiar with it. For those in the community less familiar with Kent's work, this exhibition provides a splendid study of the growth and steady evolution of an extraordinarily interesting, creative, and imaginative individual. At the same time, I expect this display to underscore a familiar irony in American art, that of the truly high quality of work produced by many artists working in the interior of this country that remains relatively unacknowledged by the writers, movers and shakers of the art world. That is not to say Kent's art is unknown over a broad arena; his extensive exhibition record attests to that. I am simply emphasizing that, like others, his achievement deserves to be even more widely honored.

Aside from the obvious enrichment for the public in viewing a broad-span exhibition of this type; imagine, if you will, how humbling, thrilling, and yet, perhaps, even terrifying it must be for the artist to confront the cycles of his own creativity covering approximately three decades of his life. I would expect each work to recall the travail leading to its existence; and, when measured in sum, I can well imagine the entire outlay thrusting upon the artist a rare opportunity to face his achievement in forceful perspective. Such moments of truth often have dramatic consequences on the future course of an artist's pursuit. It is thrilling for me to imagine what impact this exhibition will have on Kent, what revelations will occur, and how those may stimulate his outlook and work in the future.

Kent studied printmaking under me and received his M.A. degree at the University of New Mexico in 1975. Already a fairly accomplished printmaker as an undergraduate, he impressed me by his consummate craftsmanship; fresh, personable intelligence; and yet private introspective nature. Even in those early years he seemed absorbed in an imagery of intimate outlook, of exquisite surfaces and normally unappealing subjects (crushed cans, sewer lids, etc.), the detritus of civilization which he brought to our attention through such indirect, non-traditional techniques as rubbings, transfers, and erasures. In retrospect, it occurs to me that Kent's images and means of visualizing them along with the techniques with which they are conveyed were always indirect and stood oblique to the conventional contemporary practice. By consequence, they contain an intentional obscurity and haunting mystery that magnify their presence.

What are we to make of Rush's work as it moves from the incredibly delicate and silvery touch of some of his collotypes and clichés-verres to dark, dusty, grainy forms replete with scratches, ticks, pricks, and with foreboding color, varnished surfaces and blurred forms? And what of the forms depicted? We are told some are walls, pavements, curbstones, and lampposts. Some observers have likened these pictures to the experiments of pioneer nineteenth-century photographers; certainly they have the peculiar sense of time removed. Yet, on another level many have the appearance of normally invisible scientific phenomena captured in the laboratory by the electron microscope. Here we may be observing the elusive tracks of sub-atomic particles of elementary matter darting about the ribbons, clumps, and clots of unknown substances. As well, these linear zips serve to define loosely the space in which the mystery exists, while at the same time providing movement and velocity as counterpoints to otherwise, stolid immobile forms.

The difference between what is depicted and what is implied here is, of course, subjective. The prosaic object from everyday life, as identified by the title, is transported into minute or, at times, monumental scale existing in a half-lit netherworld that, for some, appears empty, forlorn, and forever elusive. For me, these pictures are continually hovering on the edges of remembrance; something known yet not quite identifiable; powerful, provocative, and deeply persuasive. Viewing this rich array of Kent Rush's art, I should think that one cannot help but feel the powerful weight of history, the erosion of time, and the ultimate challenge of the unknown.

It is also worth noting that, from the mid-1970s onward, Kent Rush has exhibited, taught, lectured, and travelled extensively. No less gifted as a teacher, he has organized workshops and touched the lives of students from Florence, Italy, to Lima, Perú and from Oaxaca, México, to his home base at the University of Texas in San Antonio. Along with being impressively skilled in traditional printmaking practices, he is one of a handful of specialists in the world who are masters of the complex technology of collotype printing. It is all the more remarkable, then, that Kent Rush has conquered the means to balance dual careers as a seriously significant artist and as a deeply committed teacher, each role complementing the other.

Garo Z. Antreasian, Albuquerque, N.M., 1998

Introduction and Acknowledgements

A retrospective is a major undertaking for any museum, an endeavor requiring the thoughtful and careful work of many dedicated people. It has been my great privilege to share the organization of this retrospective with a number of individuals whose dedication is matched only by their enthusiasm and professionalism. I would like to take this opportunity to thank all of those who helped to make *Kent Rush: A Retrospective* possible.

First I would like to thank the subject of this undertaking, Kent Rush. He welcomed the invasion of his life that a retrospective necessitates and he has provided assistance, advice, and expertise at every stage of the process. I am particularly grateful for his apparently innate organizational skills. His records and storage methods indicate that he could easily have become a curator if he had not chosen to be an artist. His skills in these areas helped to make much of our task easier.

Allison Hays Lane, director of the Artists' Gallery, has been invaluable in keeping the whole process of producing the exhibition's catalogue on the right track. She deftly and patiently kept everyone connected and made sure that we were all on the same page. I am especially grateful to her for arranging two interviews with the artist which gave me needed insight into Rush's life and work. Rosemary Flores and Dana L. Drocher, of Federal Court Reporters, generously donated their services, thereby making those interviews more efficient and productive. I wish to thank her as well for enlisting the invaluable assistance of Susan Kaufman who served as editor of the catalogue.

It has been a pleasure to work with everyone at Command P. Chuck Maurer, DeLinda Stephens, Dan Gipp, and Roslyn Walker have done a great job of supervising the production of the exhibition catalogue. As he did for the two previous catalogues in this series, Mr. Maurer has again made a generous contribution of his and his staff's time and expertise to make the project a reality. I am also very grateful to Carrie Phillips of Clampitt Paper Company for working with Command P and the McNay to produce such a beautiful catalogue.

Michael Jay Smith, who does so much work for the McNay that he seems a part of our staff, was responsible for all but one of the photographic illustrations in the catalogue. The exception is the portrait of the artist. The author of that portrait must admit that it simply does not measure up to Mr. Smith's exacting standards.

My colleagues at the McNay have contributed greatly to the success of this endeavor. I would like to thank Bill Chiego, McNay director, for giving me the opportunity to organize one of the shows in our retrospective series. I am also grateful to Ed Hepner, Patric Cormier, and Nancy Orr, preparators; Rose Glennon, curator of education; and Marti Alpard, development director. My heartfelt thanks go to Heather Lammers, collections manager. She handled all of the loans for the exhibition, generated the first checklist, and, in general, made my work on this project easier and more pleasant.

Of course, I wish to express my gratitude to all of the lenders to the exhibition. Many of them were understandably reluctant to lend these beautiful and compelling works. I greatly appreciate and understand the sacrifice the lenders have made by temporarily letting go of their treasures. I hope and trust that they will agree with me that it has definitely been worth it.

Lastly, and most importantly, I want to thank Barbara and Harold Wood for making this series of retrospectives possible. I greatly admire their clear vision and rare commitment. Mr. Wood's enthusiasm, in particular, has been most welcome and infectious. We are all enriched by his passion for art.

Lyle W. Williams, Curator of Prints and Drawings

Kent Rush: Life And Work

Introduction

When I arrived in San Antonio in 1992, one of the artists whose works first struck me as having integrity and depth was Kent Rush. The first pieces I saw by him were large-scale photographs of ordinary objects such as a chair or a curb (cat. 32,38). Initially, the subject matter was unimportant. More memorable and impressive were the monumental compositions themselves and the subtle variations of tone, line, and texture in which the artist reveled. Layer upon layer of marks, tonalities, scratches, media, and material betrayed the seemingly simple works as having been created in an intensely laborious and difficult way. The works also seemed to defy easy interpretation. Yet, the scale and presence of these works demanded one. They were objects that challenged the viewer to develop an individual interpretation. Like any good work of art, Rush's large-scale photographs defied being explained with a single sentence or phrase. Rather, they lent themselves to as many different meanings as there were people to view them.

Kent Rush's thoughtful and careful approach to the formal elements of art, the rigorous intellectual questions he raises and explores in his many different and rich media, and, of course, the absolute physical beauty he creates all make Kent Rush an excellent subject for one of the McNay's series of retrospectives celebrating the accomplishments and contributions of artists who have chosen to make San Antonio their home. This essay will trace Rush's development as an artist, discuss his different approaches to making art, and attempt to provide viewers with a language with which they may come to an understanding and appreciation of the work for themselves.

Childhood and College

Kent Thomas Rush was born and reared in Hayward, California, the town for which the famous fault is named. Rush remembers the Hayward hills as quite rural, only a short distance across the Bay from San Francisco. The city could easily be seen from those hills, but Rush felt that San Francisco and its culture were a world apart. Trips to the city were infrequent, but Rush did visit the Asian collections of the De Young Museum in Golden Gate Park and saw shows at the San Francisco Museum of Modern Art. His father, Melvin, was active in the community of Hayward as the industrial arts teacher at the local high school. He was a popular and respected man whom Kent knew only very briefly before his death when Kent was only six years old. He left behind his wife, Gwendolyn, a daughter, and two sons. Kent, the youngest of the three children, inherited from his father a good name and a knack for making things with the tools his father had left behind. When a gun was needed for an imaginary gunfight, it was Kent who would make it from a block of redwood. Admittedly, it is difficult to know what effect his father's premature death had on him, but it seems that the artist's introspective and independent nature might have its roots in those early years in Hayward. Certainly, his father's legacy of craftsmanship would prove very important to Rush's career.

In addition to woodworking, Rush also began drawing when he was a child. His first drawings were done on the backs of church programs to pass the time during particularly long sermons. Early encouragement came from his mother, whom Rush credits for his tenacity and perseverance, and from his grade-school teachers, who recognized his nascent ability. He was soon known as the "art kid," the one called upon when a design was needed for a school poster or flier. At Hayward High School, Rush worked on several advanced projects in a senior art class taught by Nikolaus Roukes, one of the pioneers of acrylic painting.

Upon graduating from high school in 1966, Rush had to make a decision about what to study in college. In an attempt to combine his artistic ability with his more practical math skills, he chose architecture and enrolled at California State Polytechnic University in San Luis Obispo, California. Though he did well in the architecture program, he realized, during the course of the first year, that he would rather be an art student. With the help of his mother and a job at the parks department working as a draftsman, mapmaker, and photographer, Rush began his studies at the California College of Arts and Crafts in Oakland. Having come from a family of teachers–his father and mother were teachers–and having admired the lives of his professors at college, Rush's goal after art school was to become an art professor.

As an art student, Rush concentrated his work primarily in the printmaking studio of the school. Unlike most young, idealistic art students who want to work on monumentally-scaled canvases as soon as the opportunity presents itself, Rush was attracted to the smaller, more intimate field of printmaking for a number of reasons. According to Rush, "there was something about the detail and the texture (of printmaking) that really sold me." As a child, Rush had collected insects and stamps. Both of these hobbies have something in common with printmaking and with Rush's work in general. They all require careful, thoughtful, and patient examination in order to be fully appreciated. Printmaking also requires the use of paper whose fragility, intimacy, and sensuality have made it Rush's favorite and most frequently used material. Virtually everything the artist does–from printmaking to painting to photography–he does on paper.

Perhaps as important as the predilections Rush brought to printmaking, however, was the fact that he was attracted to the camaraderie that naturally occurs in a printshop. Printmakers must work together, not only because they must use the same presses, but also because of the collaboration that is sometimes necessary to produce a print. Rush's most important print from his undergraduate days, *Untitled (Model in the Studio)* (cat. 39), demonstrates that the student had learned the technicalities of the very demanding media of etching and aquatint. More importantly, it illustrates one of the constants of Rush's work, a strong interest in rich textures and deep tonalities.

For the young man from rural Hayward, the years at the California College of Arts and Crafts were very important, not only for what he learned in the classroom, but also for what he learned in the rich cultural atmosphere of the Bay Area in the late 1960s. At school, Rush was greatly influenced by the photo-realist painter and teacher, Robert Bechtle. Though the student never adopted the style of his teacher, there was something in Bechtle's philosophy or approach to making art that Rush found appealing. Bechtle's paintings of cars and houses usually have a very distant vantage point. The artist and the viewer are completely removed from the scene being depicted. They are very quiet and still compositions as if, as Rush has said of them, the scene had been viewed through a telephoto lens. There is also in Bechtle's work a complete lack of narrative. Viewers are left to ponder these quiet scenes and perhaps develop a story for themselves. Rush was impressed with this cool distance between the artist and his work and, indeed, between the viewer and the work. Rush's emotionally cool art with its nearly complete lack of self-expression or obvious meaning certainly has a strong affinity with the work of this teacher. Another artist who influenced Rush in college was Charles Gill, also a Bay Area photorealist. It was Gill's subject matter that Rush found so interesting. Gill depicted everyday objects such as television sets in his work, thereby exploring the absurd and questioning what was acceptable subject matter for "fine art." Much of Rush's mature work would also focus on the absurd and the mundane.

Outside school, there were many other ideas for the young student to absorb and, perhaps, include in his own art. Rush attended many experimental theatre events as well as poetry readings. Beat poetry had had its day, but was still popular in the Bay Area at the time. Two Beat poets whose nonsensical works appealed to Rush were Lawrence Ferlinghetti and Kenneth Patchen. For Rush, this type of poetry would prove more memorable than the performances of the Jefferson Airplane and the Grateful Dead that he attended in those heady college days.

After graduating from college in 1970, Rush spent a couple of years doing odd jobs in California and New Hampshire before deciding to go on to graduate school. In the interim, without access to a press but still wanting to work with paper, Rush made a number of collages. This medium would become as important to the artist as printmaking during the course of his graduate school career.

Graduate School, Tamarind, and San Antonio

Entering the University of New Mexico in 1973 as an M.A. student, Kent Rush studied with the eminent American artist and lithographer, Garo Antreasian, and worked as a press assistant at the Tamarind Lithography Workshop, which had recently become a research institute of the university in Albuquerque. For Rush, this was a very rich and crucial time. As is the case with most undergraduate art students, Rush did not really have an in-depth knowledge of art history or the work of prominent living artists. He also lacked technical mastery of all the media in which he wanted to work. Antreasian, Tamarind, and the graduate school experience in general changed that. Antreasian was very much steeped in the traditions of printmaking and connoisseurship and would teach by bringing a portfolio of prints to class and discussing the prints intensely and lovingly with his students. High quality and outstanding technical accomplishment were extremely important to Antreasian and he held his students to these standards. He also opened their eyes to the works of other artists that he thought might be instructive. It was Antreasian who introduced Rush to the work of Giorgio Morandi, a still-life painter and printmaker who would have a great influence on the artist during graduate school and later. Morandi's works, with their muted colors and soft light, are marvelously quiet and still, the same qualities Rush had admired in the work of his teacher, Robert Bechtle.

Tamarind had been a catalyst to the printmaking and lithography boom in the U.S. in the early 1960s, when it was based in Los Angeles. By the time it moved to Albuquerque in 1970, other presses had been established which were considered perhaps more avant-garde, but Tamarind continued to be an important and respected press which trained many of the best printers and printmakers in this country. Working at Tamarind not only made Rush a proficient technical lithographer, it also broadened his horizons since he had the opportunity to assist artists of national importance who came to produce lithographs in the workshop. Through these contacts and through interaction with his fellow students, Rush began to develop a sense of what had been done by others and what it was he wanted to do as an artist.

Rush's first job after graduate school was to start and manage the new print program at the San Antonio Art Institute. Margaret Pace Willson, an artist, art patron, and trustee of the Institute, wanted the school to have an outstanding printmaking department. It was she who donated the money for the printshop and who paid someone to be in charge of it. Rush had been recommended for the job by a number of prominent printmakers, including Leonard Lehrer who knew of Rush's work at Tamarind. Rush's affiliation with Antreasian and Tamarind, as well as his portfolio, got him the job. During his tenure at the Institute, which began in late 1975, he worked feverishly producing lithographs at the school and working on a series of collages and drawings which were to be called the "Texas Still-life Series" (cat. 4-16).

At the same time that he was setting up the new printmaking facilities and programs at the Institute, Rush was working toward an M.F.A. degree at the University of Texas at Austin and was involved in creating alternative venues for art exhibitions in the city. He and other artists got together and organized exhibitions on a shoe-string budget in a building downtown owned by Robert Tobin. It was at this alternative space that McNay director, John Leeper, saw Rush's "Texas Still-life" collages and bought one for his own collection (cat. 4). It was the artist's first sale in San Antonio and it led to an important solo exhibition at the McNay in 1977.

Aside from the 1977 exhibition, the McNay played another role in Rush's artistic development. It was at the McNay that Rush became more acquainted with New York school abstraction, through the paintings of Reginald Rowe. Rush was always particularly impressed with Rowe's *Gate IV* (1975), a painting in the museum's permanent collection. In the late 1970s, Kent's collages and other works became increasingly abstract.

Rush moved to Los Angeles in 1979 because he had a feeling that he had reached something of a dead-end in his teaching career in San Antonio. He was not making much money and the Art Institute was not an accredited school. Rush decided "that it would be just as easy to be poor in Los Angeles as it was to be poor in San Antonio." Rush managed to get representation with the Art Space Gallery in Los Angeles, which was run by Lucy Adelman. This established a presence for Rush in an important art center which would last for a number of years. The main changes in Rush's art at this time were that he began to paint, draw, and make collages on stretched-paper panels (cat. 17) and that his work became totally non-objective.

Rush enjoyed Los Angeles and even found something redeemable about its horrible air quality. The gray atmosphere had a tonality very similar to that which he was creating in his work. However, after a year in Los Angeles, he was back in the San Francisco Bay Area teaching for two semesters at his alma mater, the California College of Arts and Crafts. While there, he became reacquainted with his former teacher, Robert Bechtle. Bechtle encouraged Rush to open up the scale of his stretched-paper panels even more than he had in Los Angeles. Rush did so, and the resulting series of panel paintings completed between 1982 and 1986 were the most beautiful works the artist had created up to that time (cat. 19-25).

In the fall of 1982, Rush left California to become an assistant professor at the University of Texas at San Antonio. Since that time, he has been crucial to the development of the university's printmaking program, helping make it into one of the best in the region. He has not made many collages or paintings in recent years, but he continues to be a very active printmaker and, since about 1986, an innovative photographer. He has continued to receive solo exhibitions of his work in venues as diverse as San Antonio, London, Oaxaca and Lima. In 1988, Rush received a Fulbright Fellowship to work and teach in México. That same year, he also received tenure at the University of Texas at San Antonio. He continues to teach and work in San Antonio where he lives with his wife, the artist Haydeé Victoria Suescum, and their son, Kent Alejandro.

Common Themes in Rush's Work

There is a progression and a method to Rush's artistic development over the past three decades which become clear when one has the opportunity to see his works from different periods side by side. Although done in different media, all of Rush's work explores issues of how an image is made and how it is read by an audience. One of the first things one will note is what seems to be a lack of color, at least a lack of color other than black and gray. Actually, there is a great deal of color in Rush's work, but it is subtle and you must look for it. Just as the meaning of the works is intentionally unclear and hard to see, so too is the color. There is a reason for this.

Color is the easiest of all the formal elements of art to appreciate. Everyone responds to color. Rush, however, is more interested in other, less accessible formal elements, especially tone, line, and texture. These elements become all the more important and visible in the absence of bright, seductive colors.

The tonality of the works–whether they are small collages, paintings on stretched paper panels, photographs, or prints–is dark, with few sharp contrasts. Like Mark Rothko and Ad Reinhardt, Rush is interested in shifts in tonality, shifts that the eye notices slowly, gradually. These are not works which were meant to be dazzling and obvious, but subtle and thought-provoking. As on the blackest of nights, forms and lines appear only once you have looked intently for a very long time. Rush achieves this same effect in many of his works (cat. 23). Because of their subtle and dark tonalities, Rush's art often has a quiet, meditative quality. The lines, however, are really what the artist uses to communicate. Rush has an amazing repertoire of lines. They run the gamut of all the possibilities of markmaking, from intense and violent (cat. 16) to calm and ordered (cat. 4). Visually tracing the lines, one can begin to see the gestures the artist used to create them. These gestures suggest the mood of the work; sometimes hesitant, sometimes bold and forceful. In addition to producing lines of such great depth and variety, Rush, like Cy Twombly, is able to create lines which are immediately identifiable as his own.

Textures are also important in Rush's work. Rush often uses the varied textures of paper–the artist's favorite and most used material–to add considerable visual interest to his works. Always careful to avoid making paper a precious commodity, Rush exploits its unique properties by contrasting papers of different weights, textures, and opacities in the same collage. Rush also introduces the textures of some other rather surprising materials into his collage compositions: lead, glass, and found objects such as gum wrappers and cardboard (cat.5). These change his works of art into pieces which question the boundaries and definitions of drawing, collage, and sculpture.

Rush, of course, explores these same formal concerns in his photography and printmaking, but in ways which these media dictate. One does not draw a beautiful and expressive line with photography; one must find such a line while looking at a subject through the lens of a camera (cat. 35). The textures must be seen through the lens as well, but Rush often manipulates the actual surfaces of his photographs with varnishes and scratches or by mounting them on sheets of metal. As a printmaker, Rush must work with the properties imparted by each printmaking media. A line drawn onto a lithographic stone and printed will have a different quality from one drawn directly onto a piece of paper. These differences attract Rush to the various printmaking media.

Early Collages

Aside from a print he made while an undergraduate at the California College of Arts and Crafts, the earliest works in this retrospective are two collages from a series of 1974 (cat. 1,2). They are an excellent place to start a careful examination of Rush's work in that they are a synthesis of just about everything the artist had learned until that time and they have elements which the artist would continue developing in later works. They are small collages on paper with graphite lines and rubbings. The collage elements themselves are found objects, such as a gum wrapper or a printed receipt. A sheet of transparent paper printed with halftone dots covers each collage, imparting an overall, uniform tone which prevents the collage elements from contrasting too much with the stark, white paper below. In one of the collages (cat. 1), the gum wrapper is actually a rubbing of a gum wrapper, while in the other (cat. 2) the wrapper is real. The artist seems to be playing with these simple, unpretentious elements in a way that is strongly reminiscent of the non-sensical poetry he read in college. More importantly, these two collages are formal exercises which extoll the integrity of form that everyday, mundane objects sometimes have for those who care to see. What makes these works successful is that there is a synthesis between the common objects in the collages and the simple, straightforward way in which they are presented. The artist did a series of photolithographs inspired by the subtlety and intimacy of these collages for his M.A. thesis project in 1975 (cat. 40-42).

One of the important series of works that Kent Rush has produced is the "Texas Still-life Series" (cat. 4-16). The series, comprised of works in different media, such as graphite drawings, collages, and even cast paper, is not as uniform as some of his suites, yet it contains some common elements. Most are small-scale and intimate. The still-life objects depicted are lined up horizontally across the sheet of paper just a little more than halfway up. Below this line can be vast expanses of pristine paper or other marks and scratches that activate the space. This structural quality in the composition seems to have a certain relationship to the carefully controlled compositions of the Italian still-life painter, Giorgio Morandi, an artist whom Rush has long admired.

All of the works display an incredible attention to materials, tone, texture, and line. They are very sensuous works in which the eye caresses the dark color and smooth, cool texture of lead (cat. 10), the soft, creamy white of paper, and the shiny build-up of layer upon layer of graphite. There is, of course, the still-life element, the artist's depiction of objects lying around his studio. Some of the works are literal, meaning that one can see identifiable, everyday objects such as pots and clocks (cat. 6). Others have merely the suggestion of an object's outline (cat. 7). Still others have barely visible still-life elements and are nearly completely abstract (cat. 16). It is as if Rush became more comfortable with the formal elements of his art as he went through the series. At first, he relied on identifiable objects to hold the composition together, then abandoned, even obliterated the objects with pure, expressive lines (cat. 13, 16). It is as if the artist had grown a little restless with the series as a whole and was ready to move on to the next project. In fact, when asked what brings about a change in his work, the artist admits that it is usually a need to be challenged by something new and different.

Stretched-Paper Panels

The next artistic phase for Rush entailed a new way of working with paper and larger, more abstract compositions. When he had reached a stopping point with the "Texas Still-life Series," he started experimenting with stretched-paper panels. In this process, paper is moistened so that it becomes a bit more elastic, stretched over wooden stretchers (just like those used for paintings), and then allowed to dry. As the paper dries, it contracts, becoming very tight and smooth. He appreciated the taut, drum-like quality which prevented pencils and other markmaking tools from sinking into the paper and kept their lines and marks clean, sharp, and precise on the surface. This was very important since Rush, at the time, was becoming more and more interested in the intrinsic qualities and beauty of the formal elements of his art. He was also becoming more and more interested in the cool and reserved abstractions of his friend and colleague, Reginald Rowe.

Rush's first work on a stretched-paper panel (cat. 17) was still rather small in scale, but it is a marked departure from his previous work. There is absolutely no attempt to represent something that is not there. It is completely abstract with only the expressiveness of lines, tones, and textures to carry the composition. The lines themselves have a soft, tentative quality as if Rush was still in the process of exploring the qualities of line created by working on a taut, stretched surface. Rush has said, only half-jokingly, that the tone and color of the work, a neutral gray brown, was inspired by the overall grayness of Los Angeles.

Wanting to explore the possibilities of these panels even further, and encouraged by Robert Bechtle to work on a larger scale, Rush started making four and five panel works (cat.19-25). These pieces, which comprise what the artist sometimes refers to as the "California Series," are some of Rush's richest and most varied. The first one (cat. 19) was completed while the artist was still in California; many, however, were done after his return to San Antonio. Like the "Texas Still-life Series," they are marked by a remarkable variety of line, texture, and tone. The lines, however, become more controlled and more specific; the textures, more subdued; and the colors, more evocative.

Though they were not intended to represent anything specifically, these works are often suggestive of landscapes. In *Kale* (cat. 20), white, blue, and red lines course through areas of carefully modulated browns and greens. It is as if the lines trace the motion of fish through deep water. Reading these works too literally, however, would be a mistake. The more important, more lasting reaction to a work, such as *Kale*, is a quiet, meditative one in which the forms of the work itself–the coursing lines, the subdued tones and colors–are appreciated for their intrinsic beauty and expressiveness, not for what they may or may not represent. Rush has never formally studied Zen philosophy, but there is certainly an element of it in these pieces.

There are other Asian influences as well, perhaps gently reminding us of the artist's roots in the Bay Area. The very format of the stretched-panel paintings has a calculated affinity with Japanese screens. One collector of Rush's work even mounted her work to resemble such a screen. In works such as *Camber* (cat. 24) and *Alluvial* (cat. 22), the large, white brushstrokes have characteristics similar to the calligraphic marks in Chinese scroll painting. Rush admits that these influences were always "in the air," but it would be easy to overstate their importance.

It would also be easy to try to attempt to read something into the titles of these works. Does "Kale" refer to the perceived aquatic nature of that work? No. It is not that easy. Rush chose titles for these stretched-paper pieces because of the way the actual words sounded. "Camber," for instance, is an engineering term, usually known only to engineers. Rush, however, liked the way it sounded. When pronounced, it has the same quiet quality as the lines and subtle tonal shifts of the painting. "Kale" is a word which is pronounced clearly, succinctly, and finally, much like the lines that make a quick appearance in that work and then disappear.

Photography

By the mid-1980s, Rush had completed a number of the stretched-paper panel works and was looking for new challenges. He turned to an old love, photography. Photography had always been very important to the artist, but he had considered it a hobby or as a means to other ends. He had often used photographic elements in his collages and prints. In 1986 he decided to explore the medium more. The works resulting from this exploration (cat. 26-29) are transitional, linking the "California Series" panels to the artist's more recent photographic work.

In the two photocollages, *Overpass* (cat. 26) and *Slab I* (cat. 27), Rush combined photographs of cement freeway structures with marks and tones similar to those in the panel paintings. The marks activate the surface of the photocollages while the tones unify each composition. The photographs in both works serve a couple of functions. First, they serve as purely formal elements. The strong diagonal lines of the freeway embankments and the triangles of darkness beneath the freeway structures give the compositions a sense of rhythm and order. Second, the photographs also represent something. Unlike the panel paintings of the "California Series," these works contain identifiable objects. In this way, they relate more to the artist's earlier still-life compositions.

The question that arises is why choose to include freeway overpasses and embankments in works of fine art? Rush has spent a great deal of time, certainly more than the average person, exploring the areas around and below these structures. In fact, many of the flattened bits of metal in his earlier collages he found while exploring around busy freeways. Finding beauty in those places that commuters thoughtlessly whiz by is what attracts the artist to them. There is a certain absurdity and irony in finding beauty and formal integrity in such unlikely places, and that is what interests Rush.

Works like *410 Embankment* (cat. 28) make it clear that there is beauty to be found there. At first, this seems to be a formal and subtly beautiful exercise in light gray and brown tones and gently angled diagonal lines. Looking more closely, however, one sees that some of the lines are actually cracks and that the darker lines are actually the stains left on a cement embankment by the flow of run-off water from the road surface. There are beautiful forms here, just as there were beautiful forms in the gum wrappers he used in his earlier collages.

The next two projects that Rush embarked upon he refers to as the "Nuevo Laredo Series," and "The Oaxaca Series," (cat. 30-36). Like his other series titles, these became a convenient shorthand the artist used to refer to a number of his works which were related. The gelatin silver photographs in this series were, in fact, taken in a number of places in México, and in Central and South America. They are large-scale photographs mounted onto aluminum panels. They represent common objects, like a chair (cat. 32) or a mop (cat. 30), but somehow these images are anything but common. The complicated network of lines and contrasting light and dark tones of *Untitled (Mop)* transform an everyday thing into an object of great formal beauty.

The objects themselves are placed in the very center of the large compositions. A haze of varnish, lines, and scratches partially obscures the objects, making them seem removed from the viewer, physically and temporally. The scale of the photographs, their hierarchical compositions, and their mysterious atmospheres compel the viewer to try to determine their meaning. Like Rush's other work, however, finding that meaning is not so easy.

The photographs were taken with a very inexpensive Diana camera which has a plastic lens. The artist's use of this rather crude, low-tech instrument is what accounts for the rough, unfocused quality of the images. It also accounts for the ring of black around some of the images as well as much of the hazy tonality that shrouds them. The use of this camera gives the works the quality of being from a different time and place. Despite, or because of this perceived distance, there is something about the photographs that triggers one's memory. Looking at them is a lot like looking at nineteenth-century daguerreotypes or an old family album. Our familiarity with looking at such images makes these photographs less about the artist's expression and more about the memories and reactions that we, as viewers, bring to them. The artist gives the viewers just enough to interest them visually and then pulls back to allow the viewer to determine their meaning.

For the artist, the photographs are tools to explore some of the issues that have been constant in his work for nearly three decades. There is first of all a dichotomy between the snapshot quality of these images and the undeniable presence they have as works of art. For Rush, these images represent the same questioning, manifested in his earlier works, of low and high art, the mundane and the profound.

One of the most striking works in the series is titled *Mojón* (cat. 31). The photograph is of a rounded cement column in a nondescript landscape. The fact that the artist has made the effort to take a photograph of this object, place it in the very center of the composition, and print the negative on such a large scale gives the object a certain importance. The photograph becomes a document of some monumental and sacred site that we have seen countless times in *National Geographic*. Perhaps it is a *siva lingam* in a Hindu temple. It is actually a property marker like thousands of others lining roads in México. The slang name for such a marker is "mojón" or, loosely translated, "pile of dog droppings."

Rush's most recent photographs belong to a yet incomplete group of works he calls the "New Texas Series" (cat. 37,38). Unlike the "Nuevo Laredo" and "Oaxaca Series," this latest group of work consists of pure, straightforward photography. The artist has not varnished, scratched or drawn lines on the surfaces. Rather, he has let the images stand on their own. Just as he became comfortable with the formal elements of his early collages and let them become more and more abstract, he has now become more comfortable with the medium of photography.

The subject matter of these recent works are the same freeway embankments and other cement objects that have long interested the artist. On a fall afternoon in 1997, Rush called me and invited me to go on a photo shoot with him. I was to take a portrait of Rush using one of his Diana cameras for the frontispiece of his retrospective catalogue. I was also to discover for myself why he chooses the subjects he does.

We drove down roads one would not choose to take for a Sunday drive: Perrin-Beitel, the access road to Loop 410, roads that were built solely to get from point A to point B. Our first stop was a cement culvert beneath Austin Highway, right in front of the Sunset Funeral home. With cars speeding by, Rush and I walked around the culvert trying to find its good side, an interesting perspective or backdrop for his portrait. We were unsuccessful. Our next stop was an immense drainage ditch behind a shopping center on Harry Wurzbach. The massive cement walls of the ditch were streaked by run-off with surprisingly beautiful lines. My eyes were beginning to adjust to seeing beauty in such unlikely places.

We wound up at another drainage culvert right next to the parking lot of the Galaxy Theatre. Walking up to the culvert, I saw its perfectly square openings and, much to my surprise, said "Wow, those are some nice forms." Rush replied, "Now you're getting it." That is where we decided to take the artist's picture standing in front of those black voids with the traffic going by.

Kent Rush and the Painter-Printmaker Tradition

Kent Rush belongs to what the French call the peintre-graveur (painter-printmaker) tradition, a centuries old and time-honored tradition in which artists create both paintings and prints on the same level of craftsmanship and artistic integrity. Rush does not make prints in order to produce a mere copy or a reproduction of one of his paintings, collages, drawings, or photographs. Rather, printmaking for Rush is a means to explore the formal capabilities of the various printmaking techniques while expanding upon concepts developed in other media. His prints, therefore, give his already impressive body of work additional depth and range.

Rush is very eloquent in discussing his love of printmaking and describing what he calls the "sensuality" of actually holding a print in one's hands and examining the fine lines of the print on the surface of a beautiful sheet of paper. In this way, his graphic works become intimate versions of his much larger (and more public) paintings and photographs. Their smaller scale does not, however, diminish in any way their power.

Rush has produced prints during virtually every phase of his career and artistic development. His printmaking activities have been simultaneous with his work in other media. For instance, at the same time the artist was working on the "Texas Still-life Series" of drawings and collages, he was also producing a beautiful set of lithographs which explored many of the same issues of still-life composition, texture, and line. In the lithographs, one can see the same progression from literal representation to abstraction that occurs in the collage series (cat. 44,46). One can also see in them Rush's absolute mastery of lithography. The range of tones he is able to achieve, from the blackest black to the softest gray, gives these works a dimensional quality similar to his collages. Considering the emphatic flatness of the lithographic process, this is an exceedingly difficult accomplishment.

Rush produced some of his most beautiful prints at the same time he was working on the stretched-paper panel works in the mid-1980s. Though they are not lithographic versions of any specific work, two lithographs (cat. 49, 53) from this period are very close in form and character to those paintings. They are, first of all, abstract. Their compositions are divided into sections by lines which have their source in the gaps between the panels of their larger counterparts. Other lines course across the surface of the lithographs, drawing the viewer's eye into the composition while subtle and beautiful colors enrich the background. The subtle textures of the limestone blocks actually used to print these images also show through, providing soft and elegant tones. These tones are one of the reasons that lithography is among the artist's favorite printmaking media. In a way, these lithographs are even more tantalizing than the panel paintings. Perhaps it is their smaller scale that allows the viewer to take in the entire composition all at once.

One thing that is sometimes difficult to appreciate in some of Rush's abstract prints is the artist's wonderful draftsmanship. Yet when confronted with a lithograph like *Bola de Hilo* (cat. 58), even a novice can get a sense for the beauty Rush is capable of achieving with a lithographic line. The complicated mass of lines, intersecting and weaving their way around each other, beautifully describes and represents a ball of twine. They are drawn with the same careful intent and precision as the lines in Rush's abstract prints.

Rush's most challenging prints are his collotypes. This media combines the artist's dedication to printmaking with his love of photography. In the collotype process, Rush uses negatives, the very ones used to print his large-scale photographs, to expose a light-sensitive collotype gel. When exposed, the gel hardens into tiny reticulated patterns of lines. These lines are then inked and printed. The outcome is a print of the negative created with a pattern of lines so small and fine that they impart an even, overall tone to the image (cat. 66). It is the unique quality of tones achieved by the collotype process that appeals to the artist.

It may seem that this process only complicates Rush's work unnecessarily. The question becomes why not just take a photograph and be satisfied with that? The answer is that any good artist must always explore new media while at the same time pushing the boundaries of the old. It is only through this process of experimentation that an artist's work evolves and develops. For Rush, printmaking provides many different avenues for this necessary experimentation.

Lyle W. Williams, Curator of Prints and Drawings

Lenders to the Exhibition

Carol and John Fisch, San Antonio, Texas

Maryanne Leeper Gill, San Antonio, Texas

Mr. and Mrs. Douglas Jaffe, San Antonio, Texas

Hare and Hound Press, San Antonio, Texas

Marion Koogler McNay Art Museum, San Antonio, Texas

Guillermo Nicolas, San Antonio, Texas

Libby and Alexander Oppenheimer, San Antonio, Texas

Haydeé Victoria Suescum and Kent Rush, San Antonio, Texas

Jane and Arthur Stieren, San Antonio, Texas

Adair Sutherland, San Antonio, Texas

Marie and Pic Swartz, San Antonio, Texas

Tinka and Lewis Tarver, San Antonio, Texas

Jan Tips and Reginald Rowe, San Antonio, Texas

Robert L. B. Tobin, San Antonio, Texas

JoAnn and Herman Wigodsky, San Antonio, Texas

C. Thomas Wright, San Antonio, Texas

and anonymous lenders

Checklist

Early works - collages, drawings

1.*
Untitled 1974
Collage with halftone sheet, graphite
and found object on paper
17 3/4 x 12 in.
Collection of the artist

2.*
Untitled 1974
Collage with halftone sheet, graphite
and found objects on paper
17 3/4 x 12 in.
Collection of the artist

3.
Untitled 1974
Collage with torn paper and
found object on paper
19 x 28 in.
Collection of the artist

4.*
Untitled 1976
Collage on painted paper with foil
and found objects on paper
22 x 30 in.
Collection of Maryanne Leeper Gill

5.*
Untitled 1976
Collage with graphite and
found objects on paper
30 x 22 in.
Collection of Marie and Pic Swartz

6.*
Texas Still Life 1977
Graphite on paper
30 x 22 in.
Collection of the artist

7.*
Texas Still Life 1977
Graphite on paper
30 x 22 1/2 in.
Collection of the artist

8.*
Untitled 1977
Collage with graphite and found objects on paper
30 x 22 in.
Collection of Libby and Alexander Oppenheimer

9.*
Untitled 1977
Collage with graphite and found objects on paper
30 x 22 in.
Collection of Adair Sutherland

10.*
Untitled 1977
Collage with graphite and found objects on paper
30 x 22 in.
Collection of Jan Tips and Reginald Rowe

11.*
Untitled 1977
Cast paper with collage and graphite
25 x 18 in.
Collection of Robert L. B. Tobin

12.*
Untitled 1977
Collage with charcoal, graphite
and found objects on paper
30 x 22 in.
Collection of C. Thomas Wright

13.*
Untitled 1978
Collage with charcoal, graphite, crayon,
acrylic and found objects on paper
28 x 19 in.
Collection of the artist

* *denotes objects illustrated in the catalogue*

14.★
Untitled 1978
Collage with stenciling, acrylic, ink
and graphite on paper
30 x 22 in.
Collection of Carol and John Fisch

15.★
Untitled 1978
Collage with stenciling, acrylic, charcoal,
graphite and found objects on panel
67 x 48 in.
Collection of Jane and Arthur Stieren

16.★
Untitled 1979
Graphite, charcoal, chalk and acrylic on paper
30 x 22 1/2 in.
Collection of the artist

17.★
California Series I 1980
Collage with graphite, ink and
colored pencils on stretched-paper panel
Collection of the artist

18.
Untitled 1981
Collage with graphite, ink, colored pencils,
chalk, charcoal and found objects on paper
29 1/4 x 20 1/4 in.
Collection of the artist

Paintings on Paper Panels

19.★
Untitled 1981
Collage with acrylic, ink, chalk, charcoal
and graphite on stretched-paper panels
60 x 100 in.
Private Collection

20.★
Kale 1982
Collage with acrylic, ink, chalk, charcoal
and graphite on stretched-paper panels
52 x 80 in.
Collection of the artist

21.★
Abut 1983
Photocollage with casein, acrylic, ink
and graphite on stretched paper-panels
60 x 100 in.
Collection of Mr. and Mrs. Douglas Jaffe

22.★
Alluvial 1983
Casein, ink and acrylic on stretched-paper panels
60 x 80 in.
Collection of Guillermo Nicolas

23.★
Anita 1983
Casein, ink, acrylic and charcoal
on stretched-paper panels
60 x 100 in.
Collection of Tinka and Lewis Tarver

24.★
Camber 1983
Casein, ink, acrylic and graphite
on stretched-paper panels
60 x 100 in.
Collection of the McNay Art Museum,
Gift of Bettie Ward
1996.29

25.★
Untitled 1984
Collage with acrylic, ink, charcoal and graphite
on stretched-paper panels
29 x 53 in.
Collection of JoAnn and Herman Wigodsky

Transitional Works

26.*
Overpass 1986
Photocollage with acrylic and ink on wood panels
60 x 96 in.
Collection of the artist

27.*
Slab I 1986
Photocollage with acrylic and ink on wood panels
60 x 96 in.
Collection of the artist

28.*
410 Embankment 1987
Toned cyanotype mounted on wood panels
61 1/2 x 84 in.
Collection of the artist

29.*
Schertz 1985
Toned cyanotype mounted on wood panels
60 x 96 in.
Private Collection

Photographs

30.*
Untitled (Mop) 1989
Gelatin silver print with varnish
and scratches mounted on aluminum panel
60 x 48 in.
Collection of the artist

31.*
Mojón 1989
Gelatin silver print with varnish
and scratches mounted on aluminum panel
60 x 48 in.
Collection of the artist

32.*
Untitled (Chair) 1989
Gelatin silver print with varnish and
scratches mounted on aluminum panel
60 x 48 in.
Collection of the artist

33.*
Untitled (Drain) 1990-91
Gelatin silver print with varnish and
scratches mounted on aluminum panel
60 x 48 in.
Collection of the artist

34.*
Untitled (Rails) 1990-91
Gelatin silver print with varnish and
scratches mounted on aluminum panel
60 x 48 in.
Collection of the artist

35.*
Untitled (Ring) 1990-91
Gelatin silver print with varnish and
scratches mounted on aluminum panel
60 x 48 in.
Collection of the artist

36.*
Untitled (Oaxaca stump) 1993
Gelatin silver prints mounted on wood panels
48 x 96 in.
Collection of the artist

37.*
Untitled (Cone bank) 1995
Gelatin silver print mounted on wood panel
60 x 60 in.
Collection of the artist

38.*
Untitled (Curb) 1997
Gelatin silver prints mounted on wood panels
48 x 144 in.
Collection of the artist

Prints

All prints unless otherwise noted are Collection of the McNay Art Museum, Gift of the artist in memory of John Palmer Leeper

39.*
Untitled (Model in the Studio) 1970
Softground etching and aquatint
30 x 22 in.
1997.4

40.
Untitled 1975
Photolithograph
16 1/2 x 13 in.
1997.5

41.*
Untitled 1975
Photolithograph
16 1/2 x 13 in.
1997.6

42.
Untitled 1975
Photolithograph
16 1/2 x 13 in.
1997.7

43.
Untitled 1977
Lithograph
30 x 22 in.
1997.8

44.*
Untitled 1977
Lithograph
30 x 22 in.
1997.9

45.
Untitled 1977
Lithograph
30 x 22 in.
1997.10

46.*
Untitled 1978
Lithograph
30 x 22 in.
1997.11

47.
Untitled 1978
Lithograph
20 x 16 1/2 in.
Collection of the McNay Art Museum, Gift of the artist
1979.21

48.
Untitled 1980
Woodcut
26 1/8 x 19 1/8 in.
1997.12

49.*
Untitled (Maroon) 1983
Lithograph
22 1/2 x 27 3/4 in.
1997.13

50.
Untitled (Sand) 1984
Lithograph
15 x 20 in.
1997.14

51.
Untitled 1984
Lithograph
15 x 11 in.
1997.15

52.
Untitled 1985
Lithograph
22 x 28 in.
1997.16

53.*
Cant 1985
Lithograph
19 1/4 x 25 1/2 in.
1997.17

54.
Untitled (Freeway) 1986
Photolithograph
22 1/4 x 30 1/4 in.
1997.18

55.
La Escobeta 1988
Lithograph on chine-collé
11 x 9 7/8 in.
1997.19

56.
El Peine 1988
Lithograph
10 x 8 5/8 in.
1997.20

57.
El Trompo 1988
Lithograph
10 x 8 in.
1997.21

58.*
Bola de Hilo 1992
Lithograph
12 1/4 x 9 in.
1997.22

59.
Mojón 1989
Collotype
20 x 15 in.
1997.23

60.
Untitled (Mop) 1989
Collotype
20 x 15 in.
1997.24

61.
Untitled (Fountain) 1989
Collotype
20 x 15 in.
1997.25

62.
Untitled (Concrete fence post) 1991
Collotype
29 1/4 x 22 in.
1997.26

63.
Untitled (Ring) 1991
Collotype
31 x 22 1/4 in.
1997.27

64.
Untitled (Rail) 1991
Collotype
29 1/2 x 22 in.
1997.28

65.
Untitled (Paint drips) 1993
Collotype
14 x 11 in.
1997.29

66.*
Untitled (Oaxaca stump) 1994
Collotype
14 x 11 in.
1997.30

67.
Untitled (Cone embankment) 1996
Collotype
22 1/2 x 20 in.
1997.31

68.
Untitled 1997
Photogravure
19 1/2 x 40
Collection of Hare and Hound Press,
San Antonio

Artist's Book

69.
Snake 1980-84
Artist's book containing nine lithographs
and collotypes with letterpress text
16 x 12 1/4 in. (book)
Collection of the McNay Art Museum,
Gift of the Friends of the McNay
1984.7.1-9

Colorplates

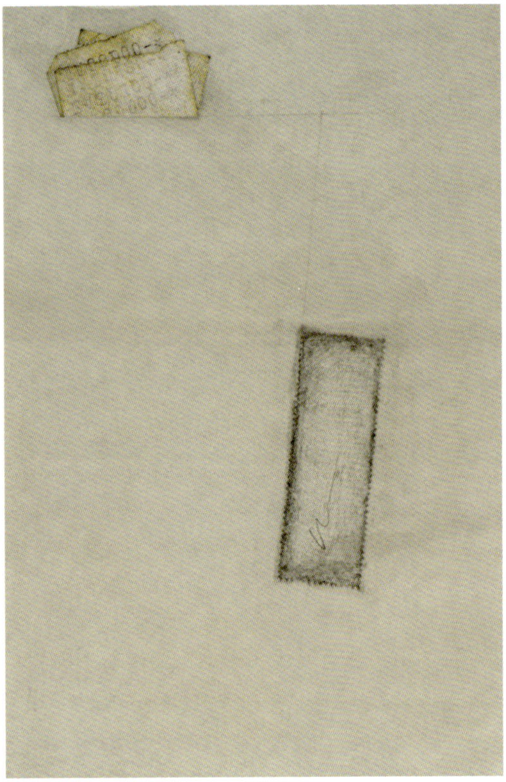

Plate 1
Untitled 1974
Collage with halftone sheet,
graphite and found object on paper
17 3/4 x 12 in.
Collection of the artist

Plate 2
Untitled 1974
Collage with halftone sheet,
graphite and found objects on paper
17 3/4 x 12 in.
Collection of the artist

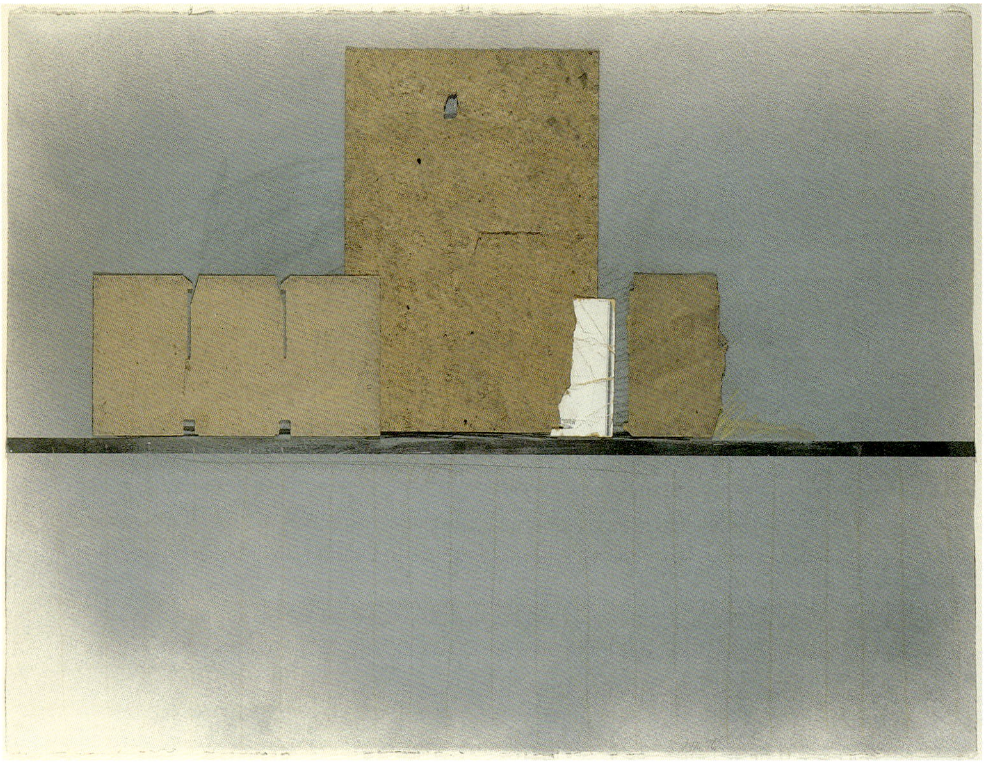

Plate 4
Untitled 1976
Collage on painted paper with
foil and found objects on paper
22 x 30 in.
Collection of Maryanne Leeper Gill

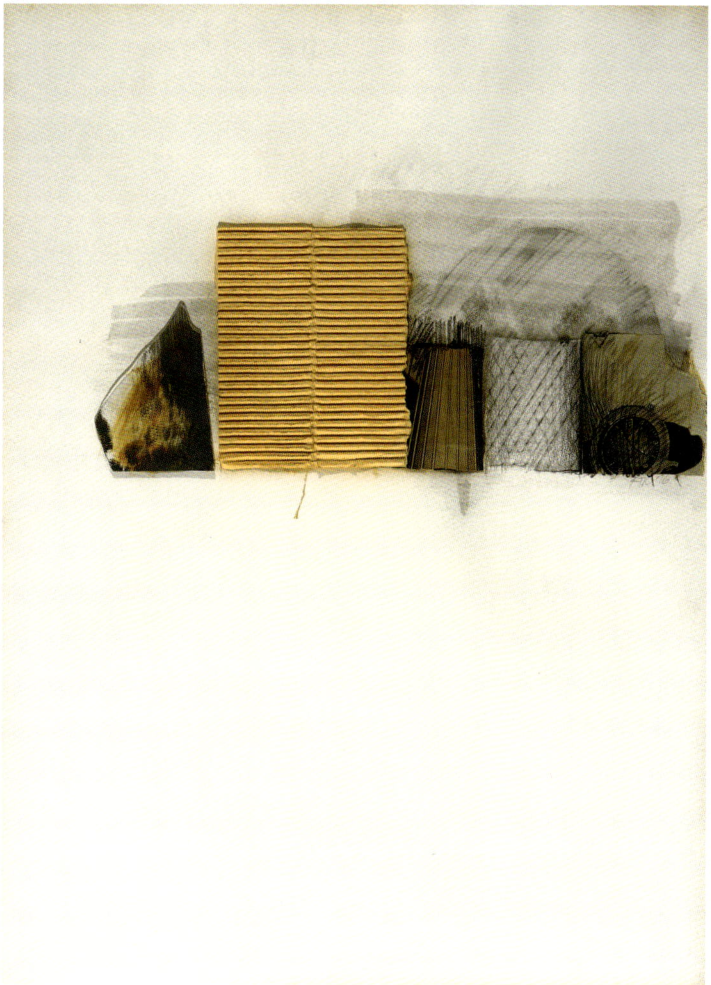

Plate 5
Untitled 1976
Collage with graphite and found objects on paper
30 x 22 in.
Collection of Marie and Pic Swartz

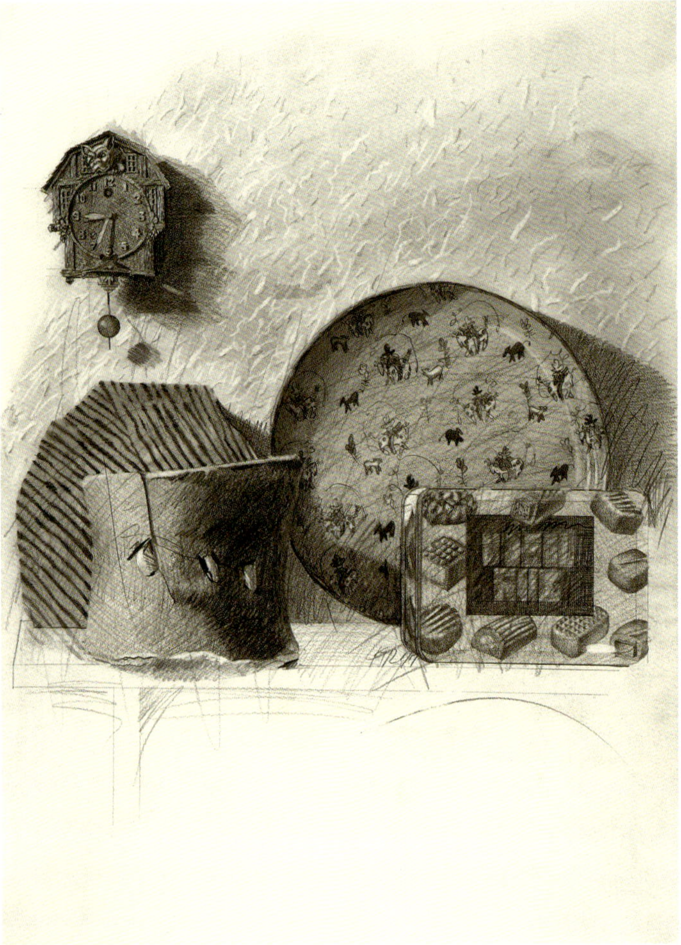

Plate 6
Texas Still Life 1977
Graphite on paper
30 x 22 in.
Collection of the artist

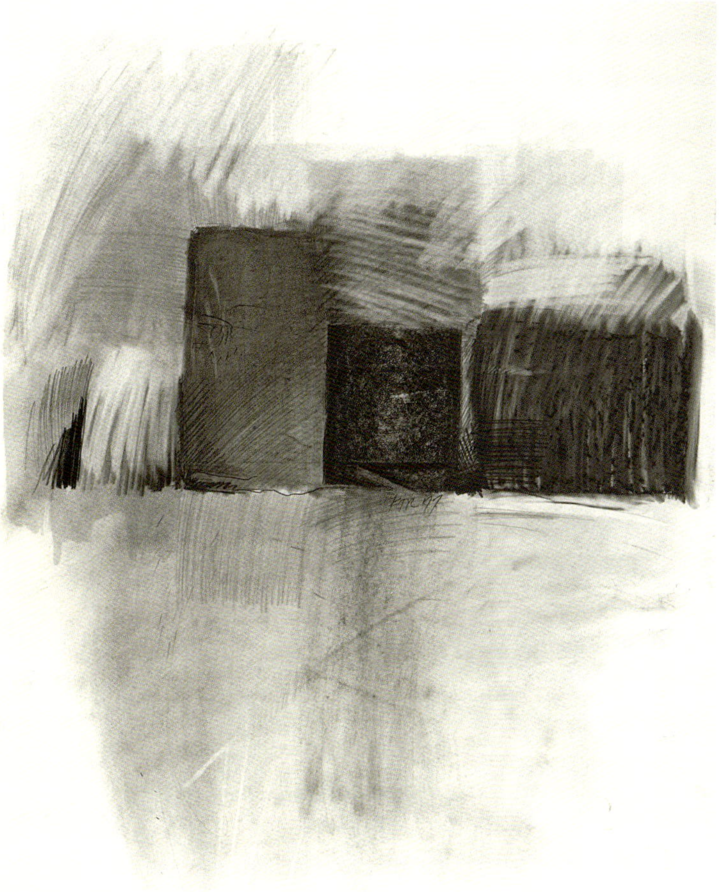

Plate 7
Texas Still Life 1977
Graphite on paper
30 x 22 1/2 in.
Collection of the artist

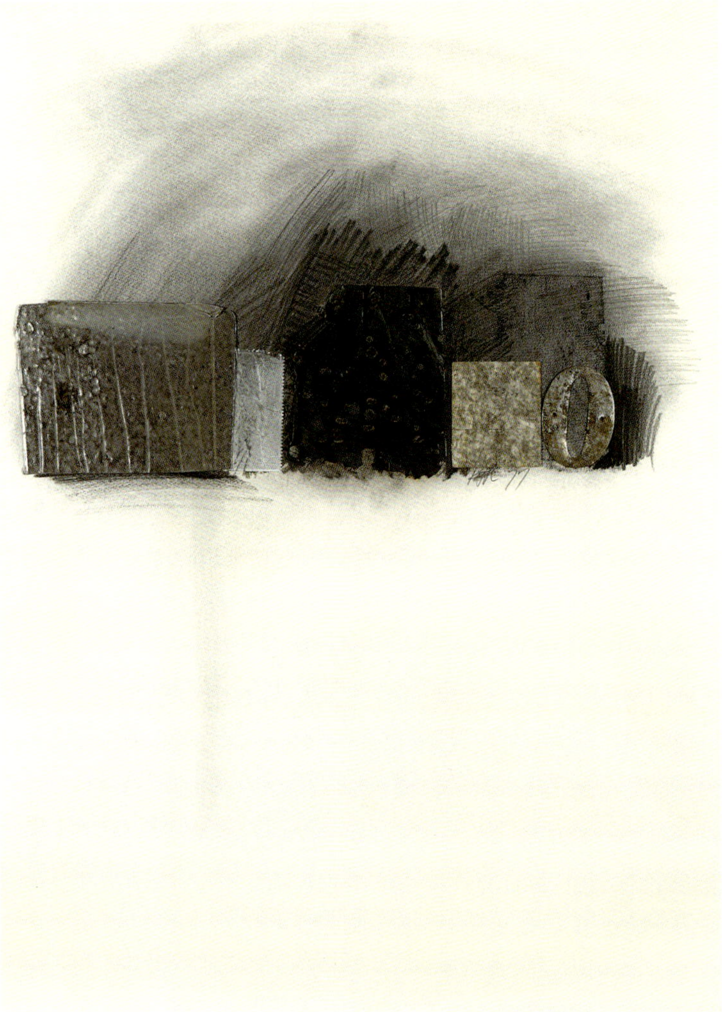

Plate 8
Untitled 1977
Collage with graphite and
found objects on paper
30 x 22 in.
Collection of Libby and Alexander Oppenheimer

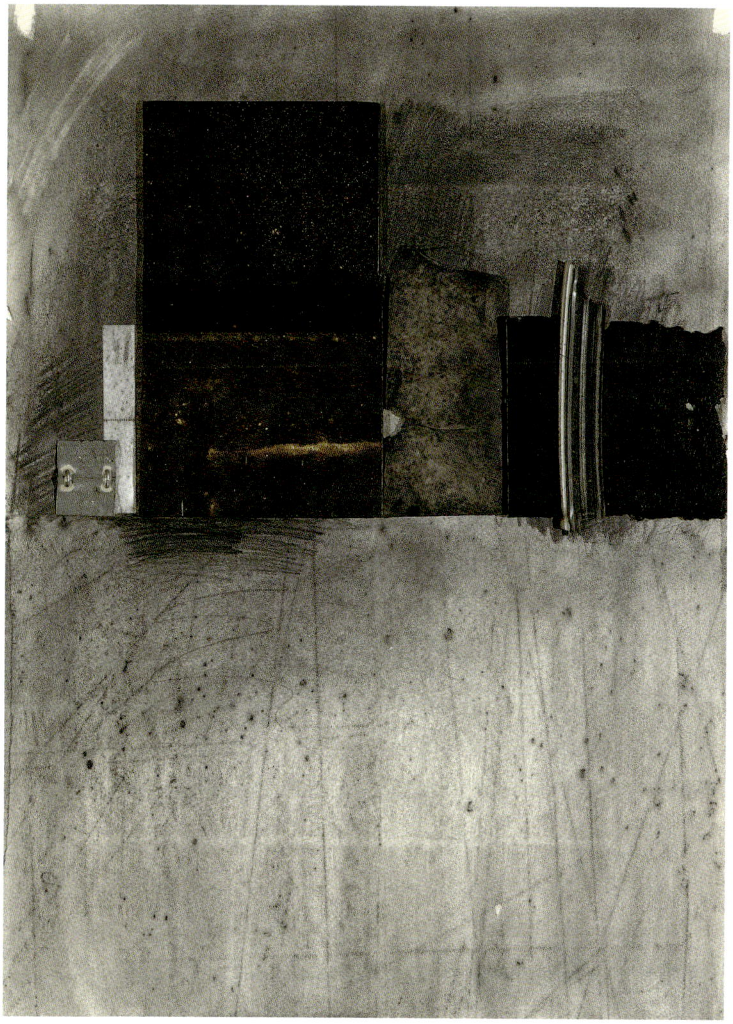

Plate 9
Untitled 1977
Collage with graphite and found objects on paper
30 x 22 in.
Collection of Adair Sutherland

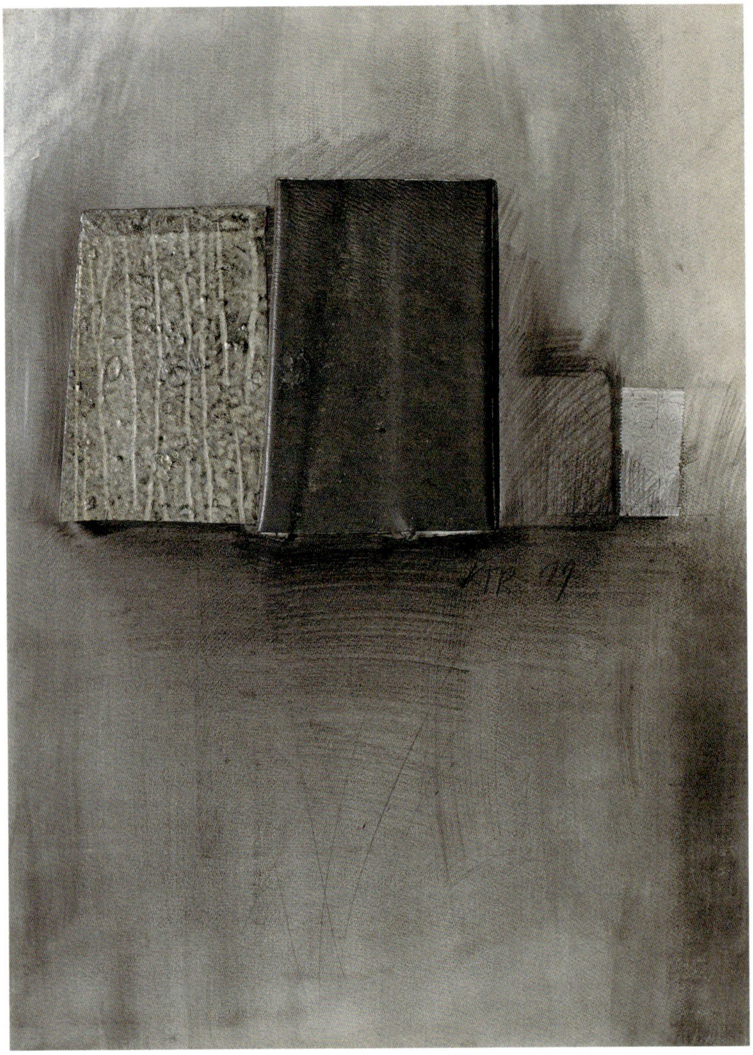

Plate 10
Untitled 1977
Collage with graphite and
found objects on paper
30 x 22 in.
Collection of Jan Tips and Reginald Rowe

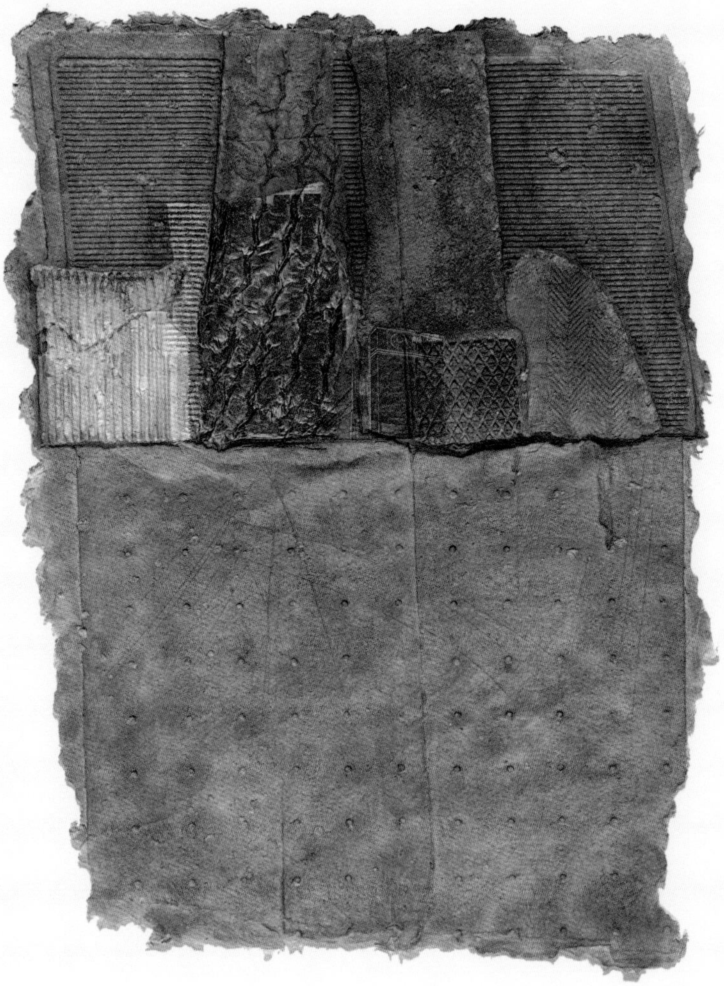

Plate 11
Untitled 1977
Cast paper with collage and graphite
25 x 18 in.
Collection of Robert L. B. Tobin

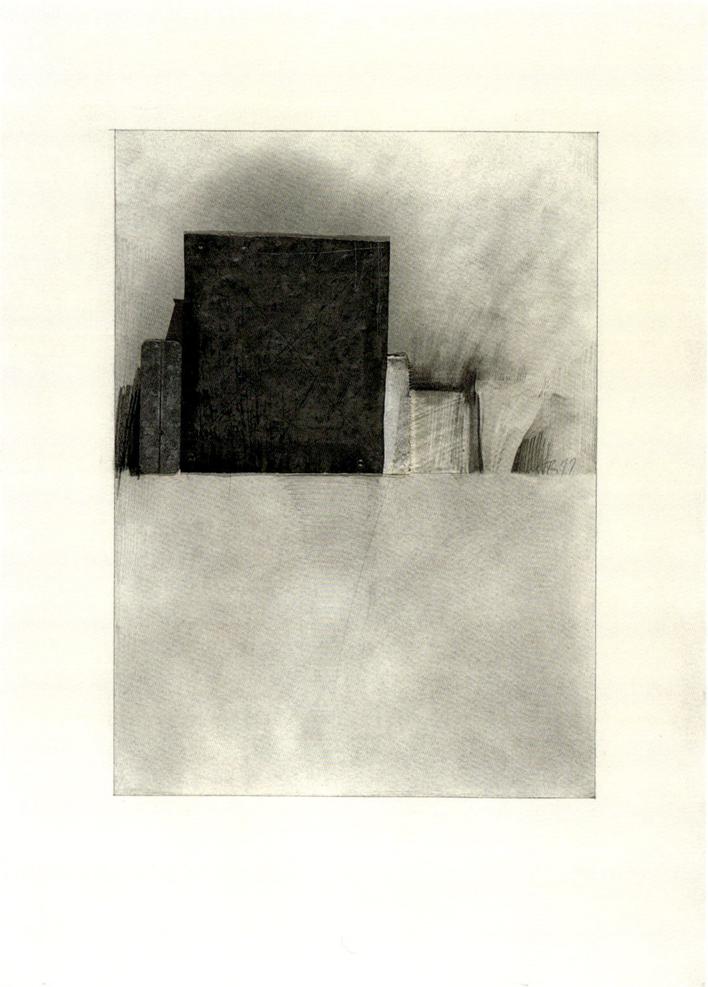

Plate 12
Untitled 1977
Collage with charcoal, graphite
and found objects on paper
30 x 22 in.
Collection of C. Thomas Wright

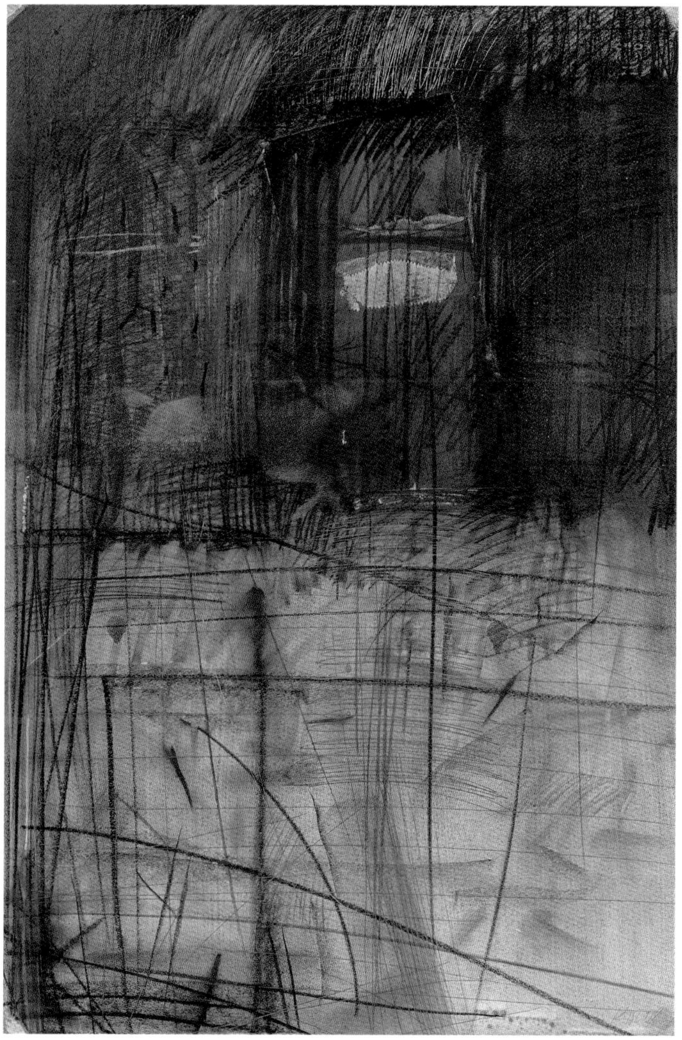

Plate 13
Untitled 1978
Collage with charcoal, graphite, crayon,
acrylic, and found objects on paper
28 x 19 in.
Collection of the artist

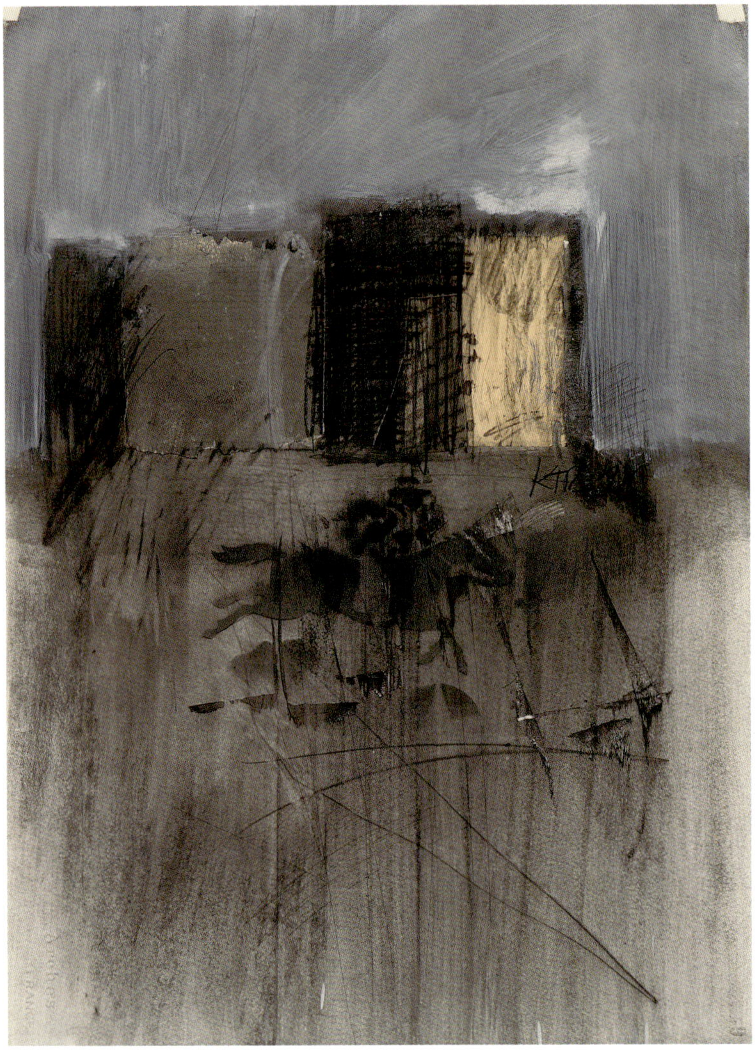

Plate 14
Untitled 1978
Collage with stenciling, acrylic,
ink and graphite on paper
30 x 22 in.
Collection of Carol and John Fisch

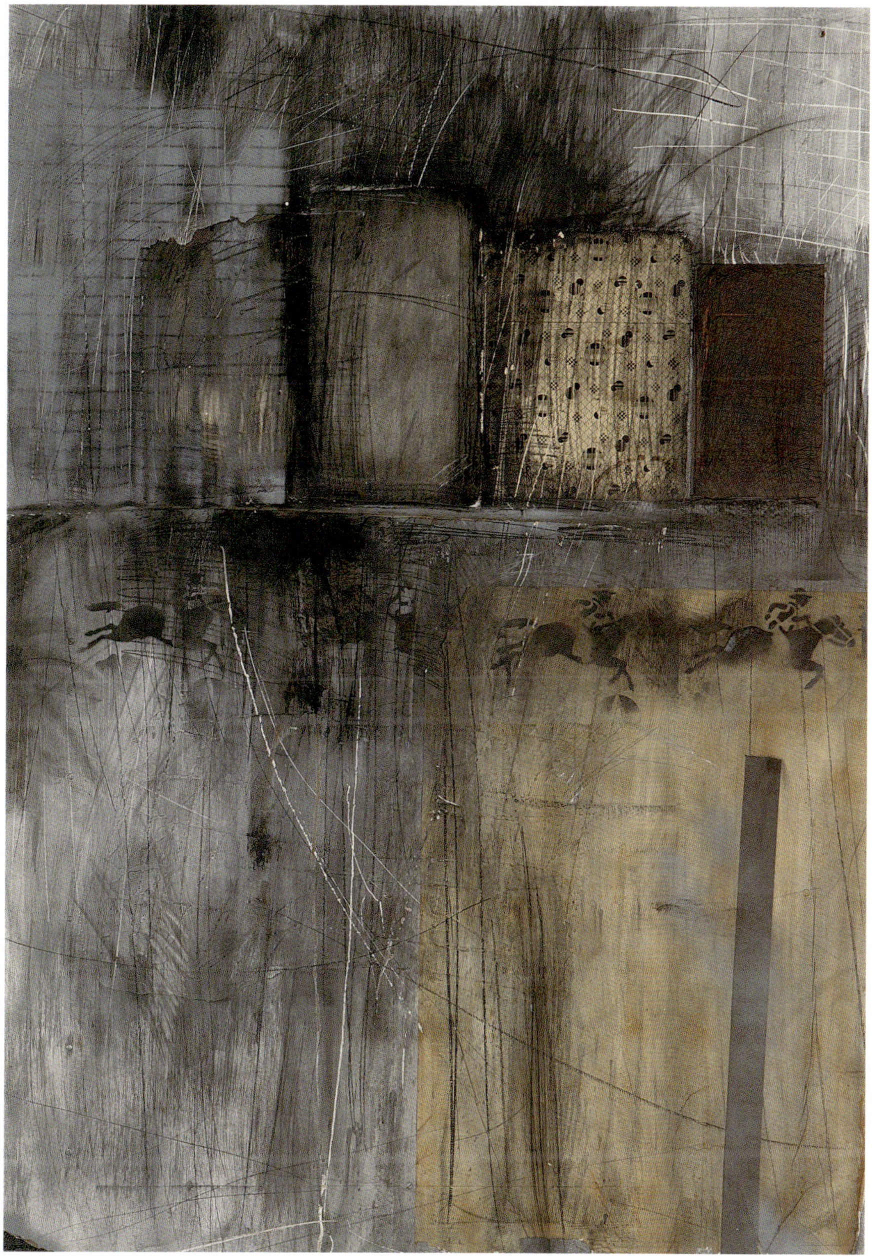

Plate 15
Untitled 1978
Collage with stenciling, acrylic, charcoal, graphite and found objects on panel
67 x 48 in.
Collection of Jane and Arthur Stieren

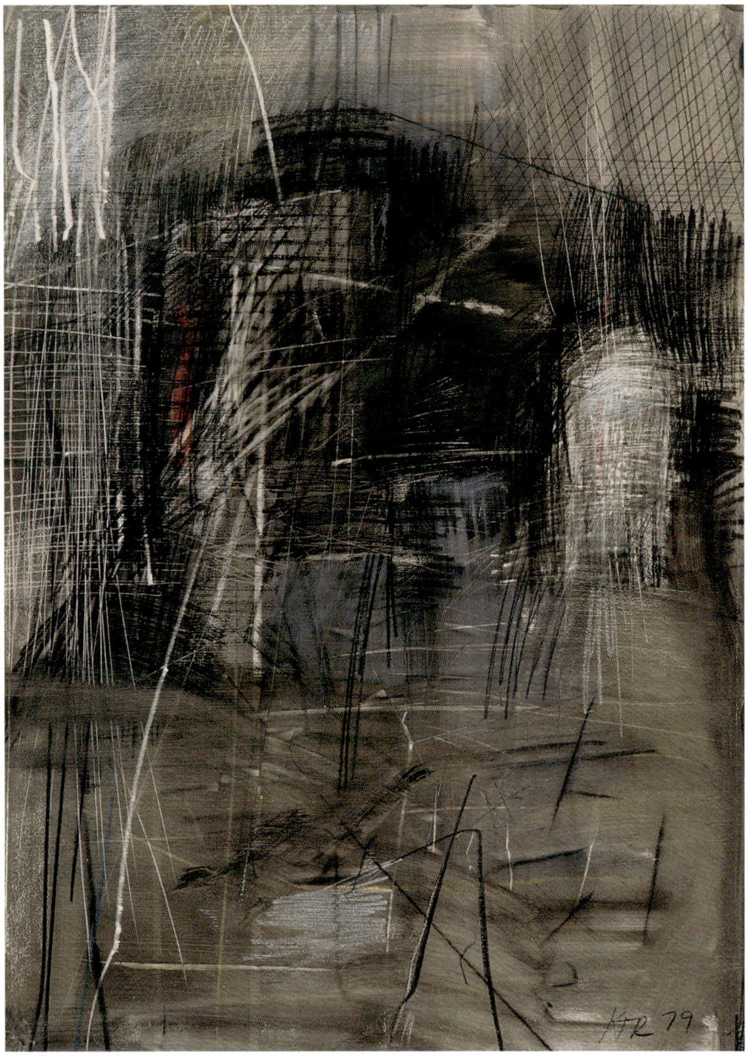

Plate 16
Untitled 1979
Graphite, charcoal, chalk and acrylic on paper
30 x 22 1/2 in.
Collection of the artist

Plate 17
California Series I 1980
Collage with graphite, ink and colored pencils on stretched-paper panel
40 x 24 in.
Collection of the artist

Plate 19
Untitled 1981
Collage with acrylic, ink, chalk, charcoal
and graphite on stretched-paper panels
60 x 100 in.
Private Collection

Plate 20
Kale 1982
Collage with acrylic, ink, chalk, charcoal
and graphite on stretched-paper panels
52 x 80 in.
Collection of the artist

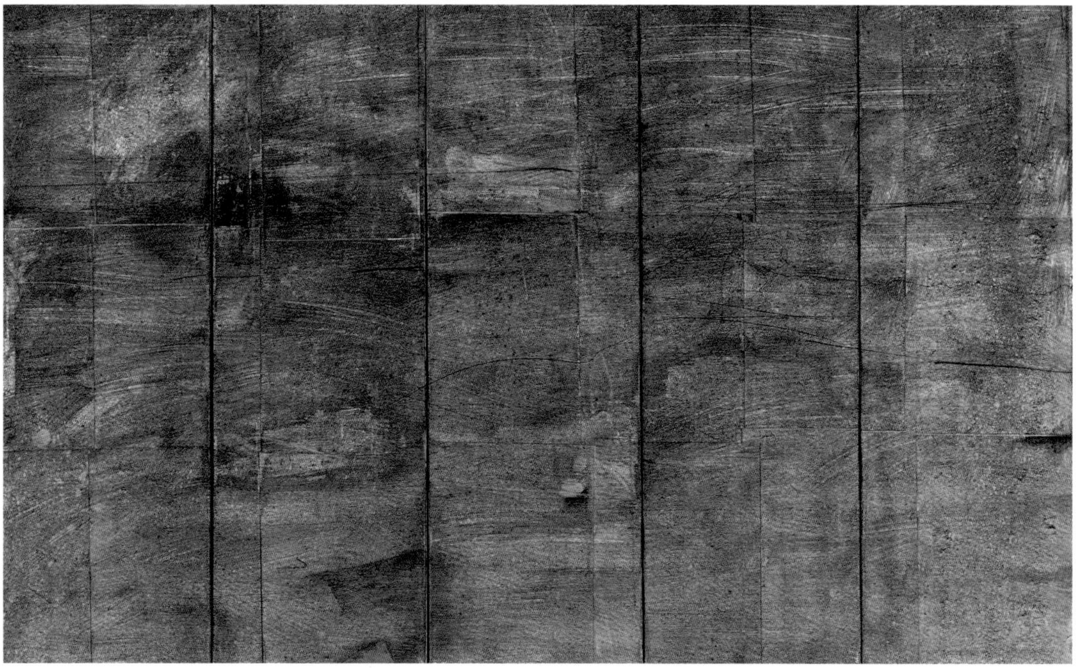

Plate 21
Abut 1983
Photocollage with casein, acrylic, ink
and graphite on stretched paper-panels
60 x 100 in.
Collection of Mr. and Mrs. Douglas Jaffe

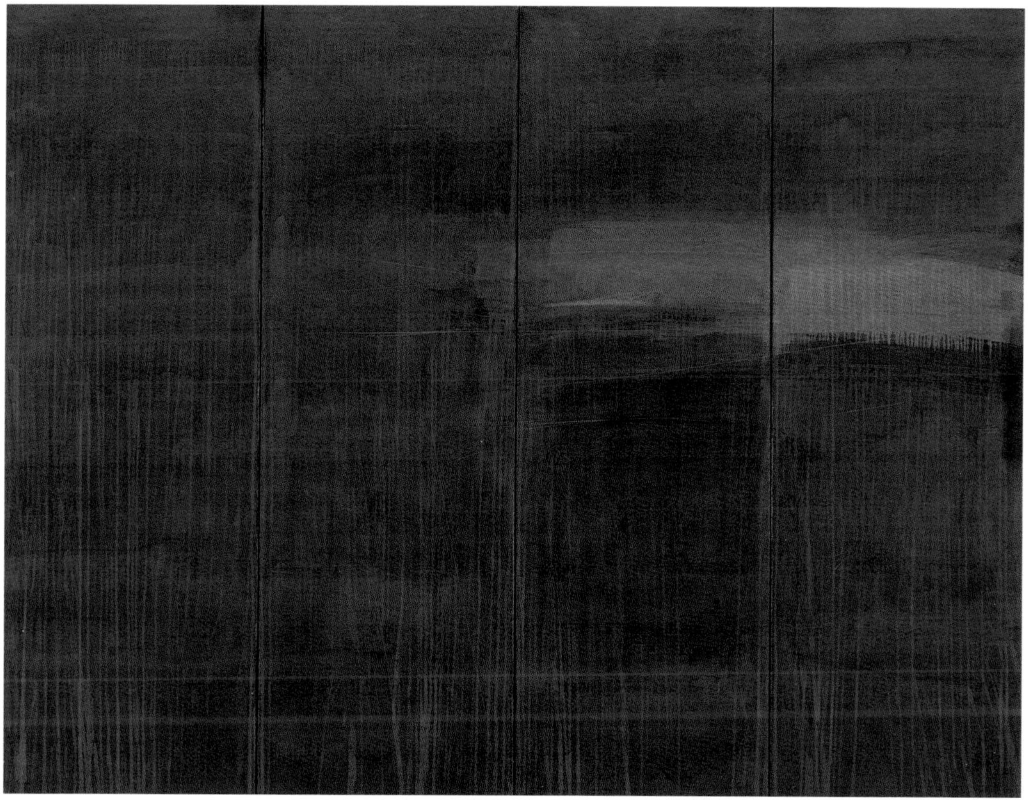

Plate 22
Alluvial 1983
Casein, ink and acrylic on stretched-paper panels
60 x 80 in.
Collection of Guillermo Nicolas

Plate 23
Anita 1983
Casein, ink, acrylic and charcoal
on stretched-paper panels
60 x 100 in.
Collection of Tinka and Lewis Tarver

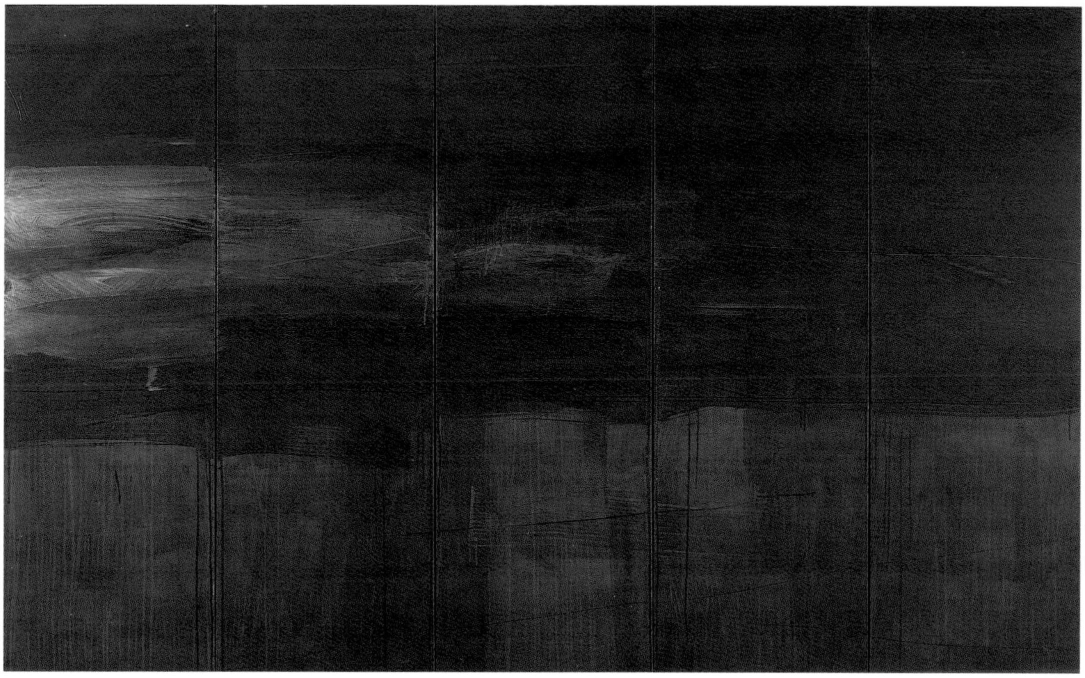

Plate 24
Camber 1983
Casein, ink, acrylic and graphite on stretched-paper panels
60 x 100 in.
Collection of the McNay Art Museum, Gift of Bettie Ward

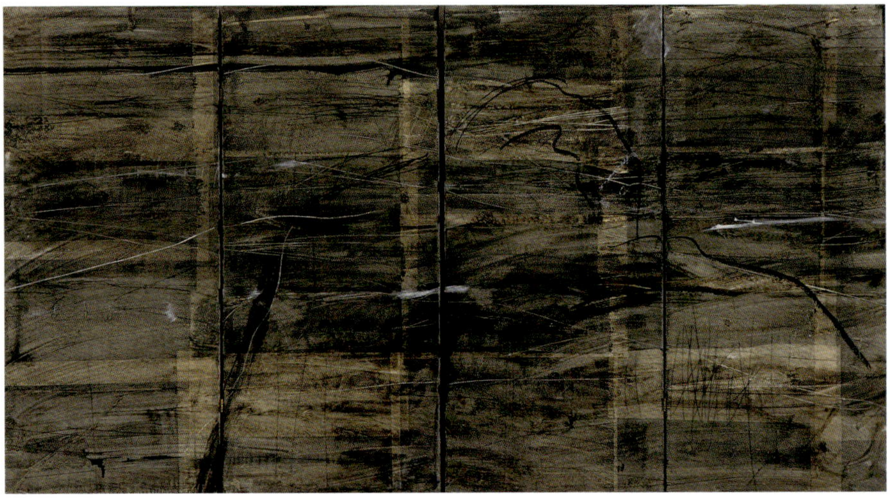

Plate 25
Untitled 1984
Collage with acrylic, ink, charcoal
and graphite on stretched-paper panels
29 x 53 in.
Collection of JoAnn and Herman Wigodsky

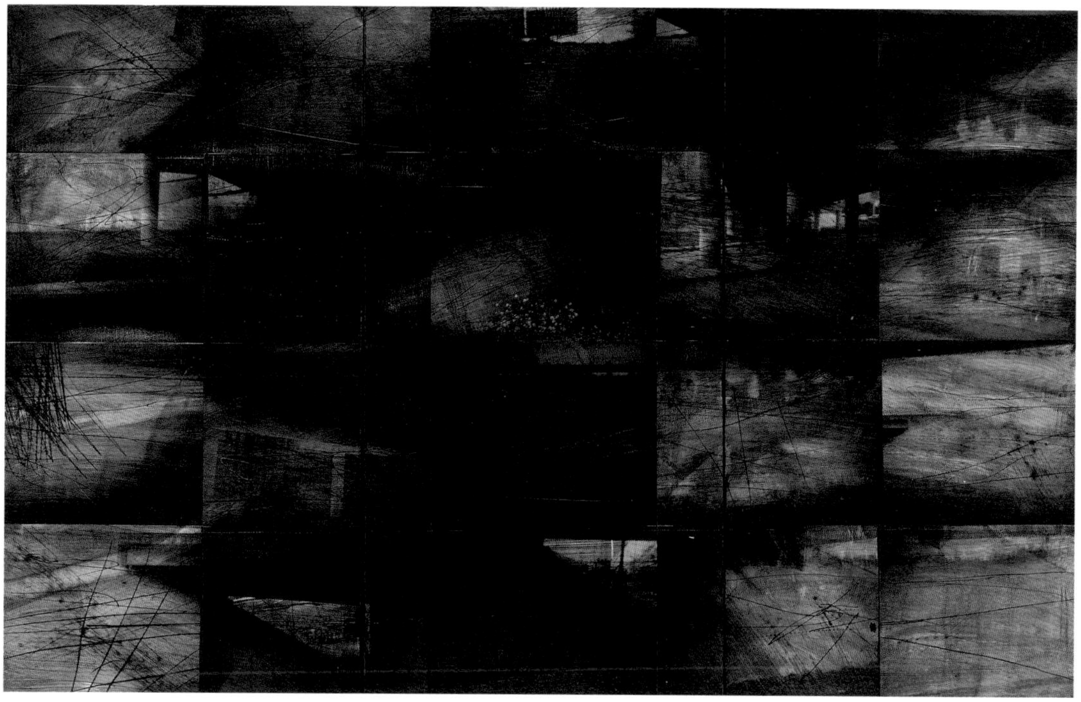

Plate 26
Overpass 1986
Photocollage with acrylic and ink on wood panels
60 x 96 in.
Collection of the artist

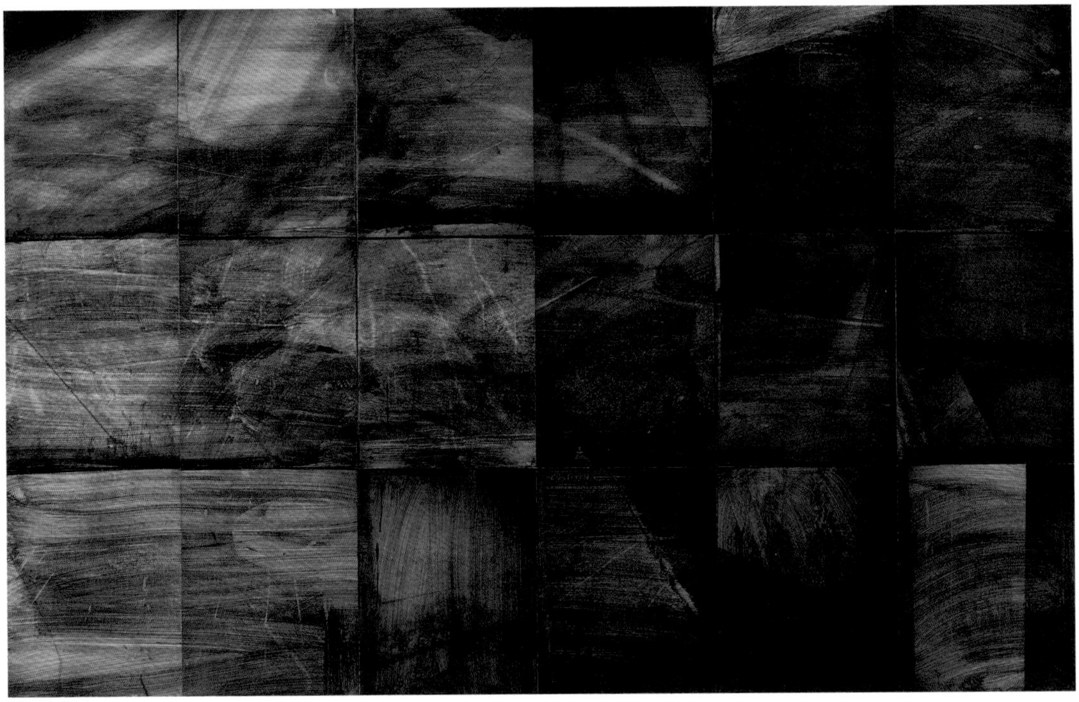

Plate 27
Slab I 1986
Photocollage with acrylic and ink on wood panels
60 x 96 in.
Collection of the artist

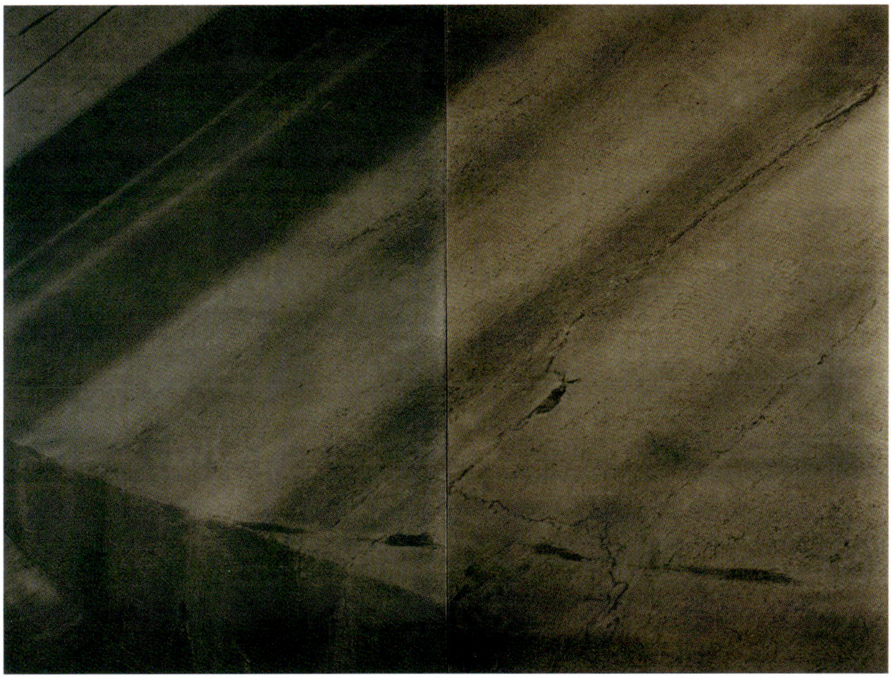

Plate 28
410 Embankment 1987
Toned cyanotype mounted on wood panels
61 1/2 x 84 in.
Collection of the artist

Plate 29
Schertz 1985
Toned cyanotype mounted on wood panels
60 x 96 in.
Private Collection

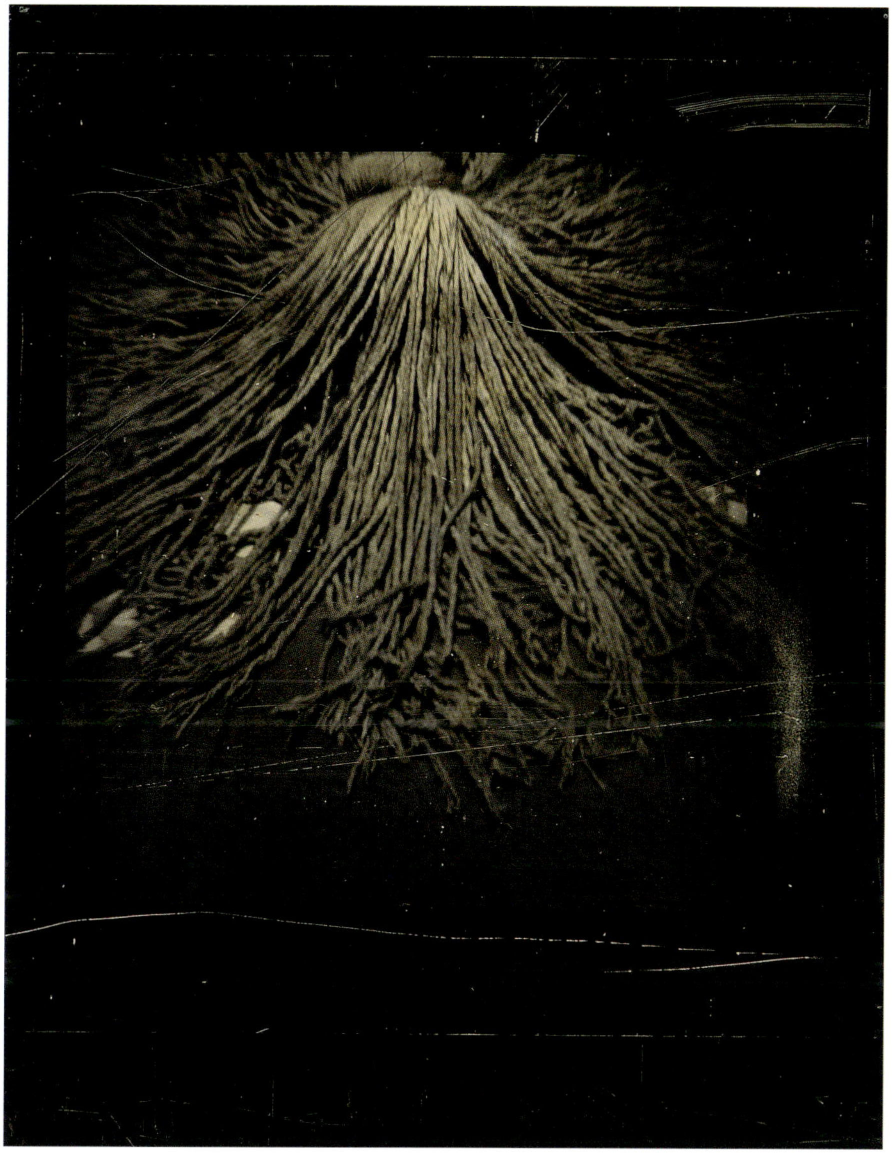

Plate 30
Untitled (Mop) 1989
Gelatin silver print with varnish and
scratches mounted on aluminum panel
60 x 48 in.
Collection of the artist

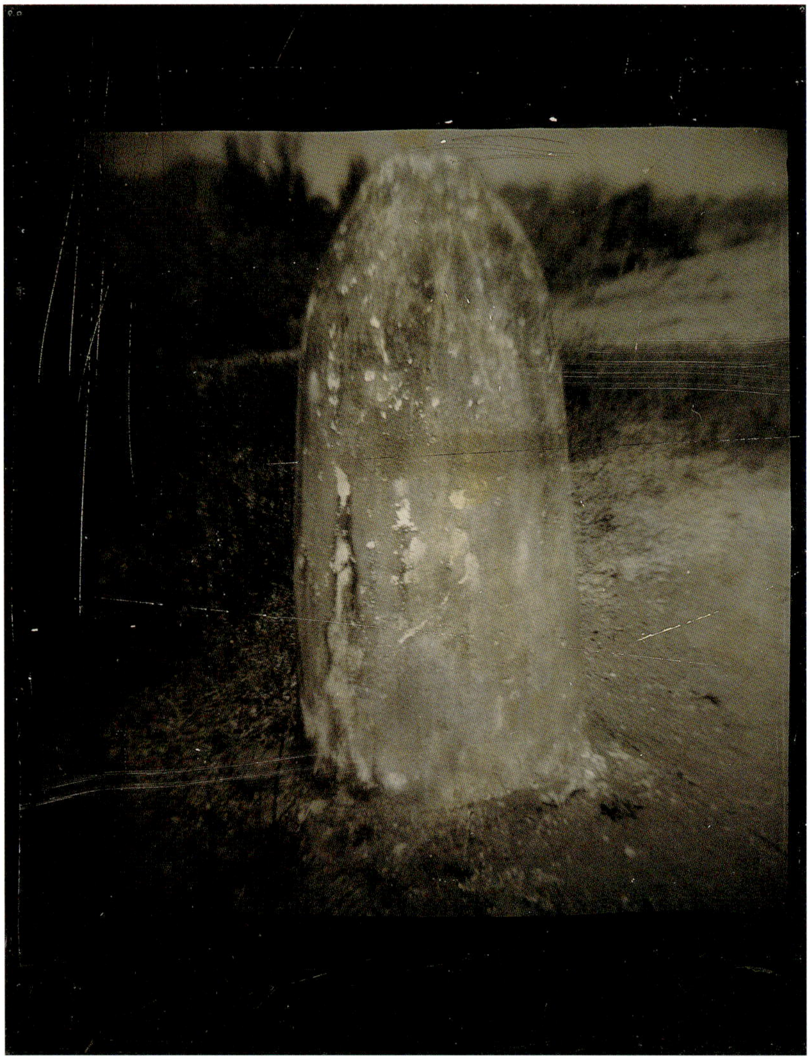

Plate 31
Mojón 1989
Gelatin silver print with varnish and
scratches mounted on aluminum panel
60 x 48 in.
Collection of the artist

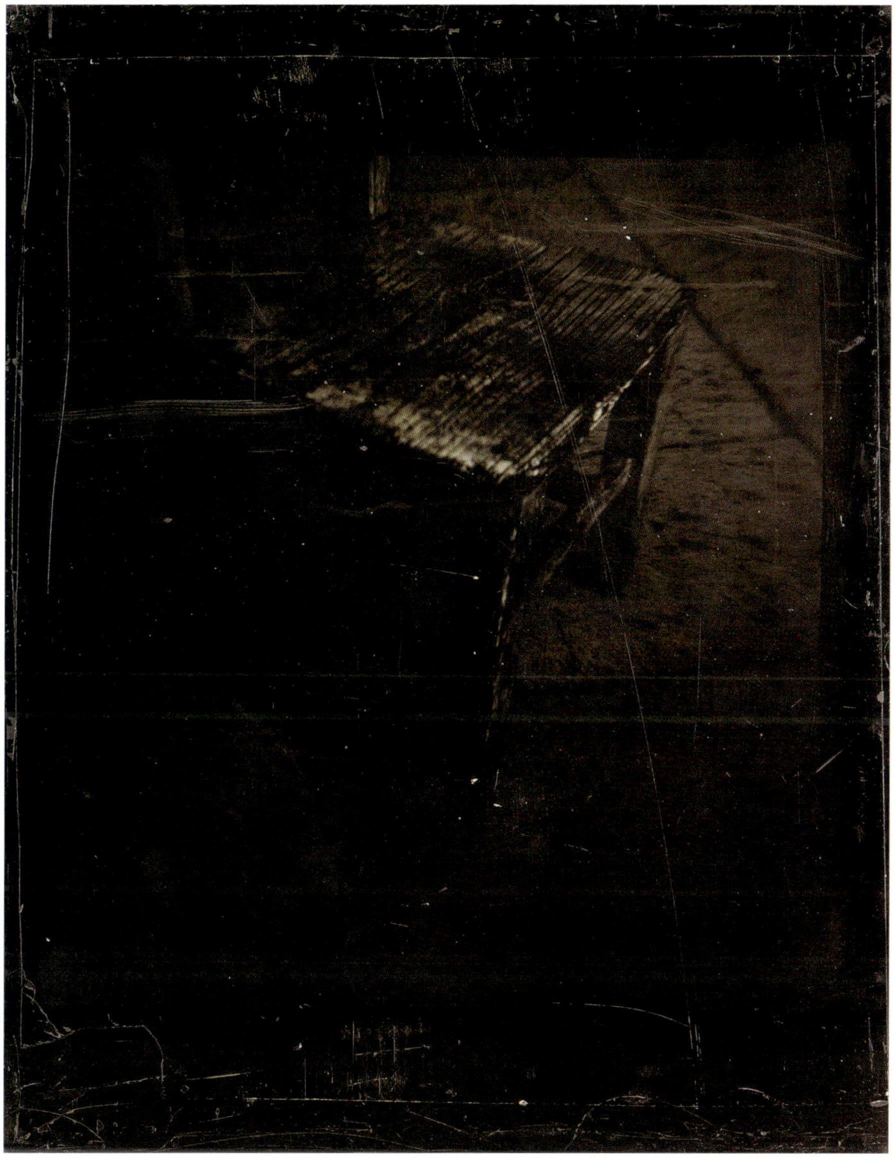

Plate 32
Untitled (Chair) 1989
Gelatin silver print with varnish and
scratches mounted on aluminum panel
60 x 48 in.
Collection of the artist

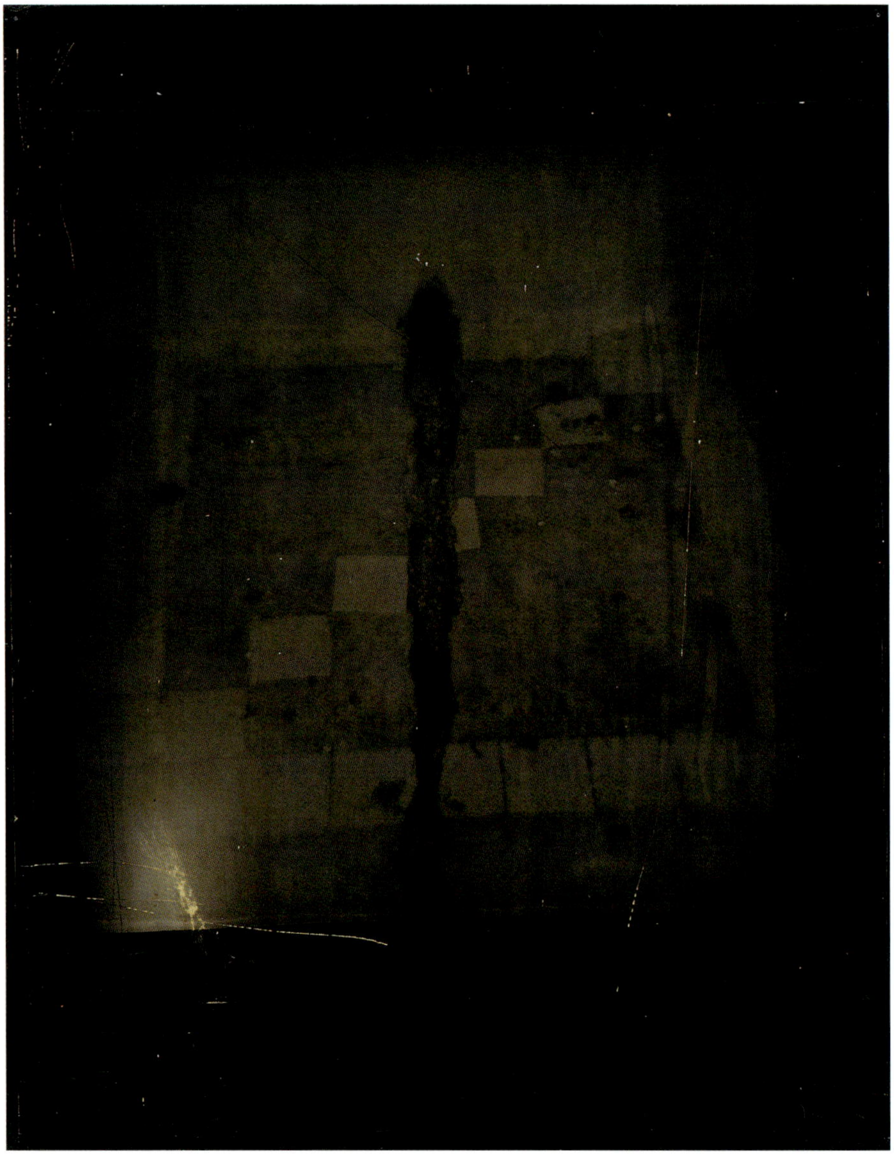

Plate 33
Untitled (Drain) 1990-91
Gelatin silver print with varnish and
scratches mounted on aluminum panel
60 x 48 in.
Collection of the artist

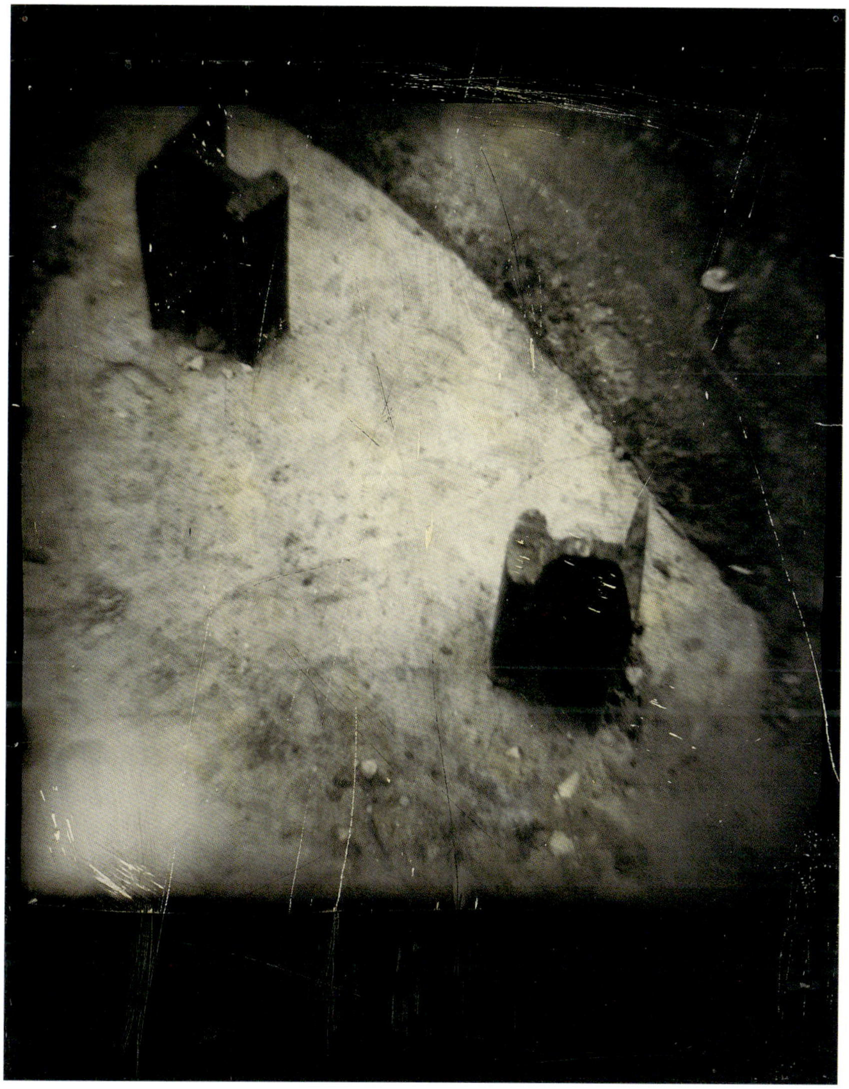

Plate 34
Untitled (Rails) 1990-91
Gelatin silver print with varnish and
scratches mounted on aluminum panel
60 x 48 in.
Collection of the artist

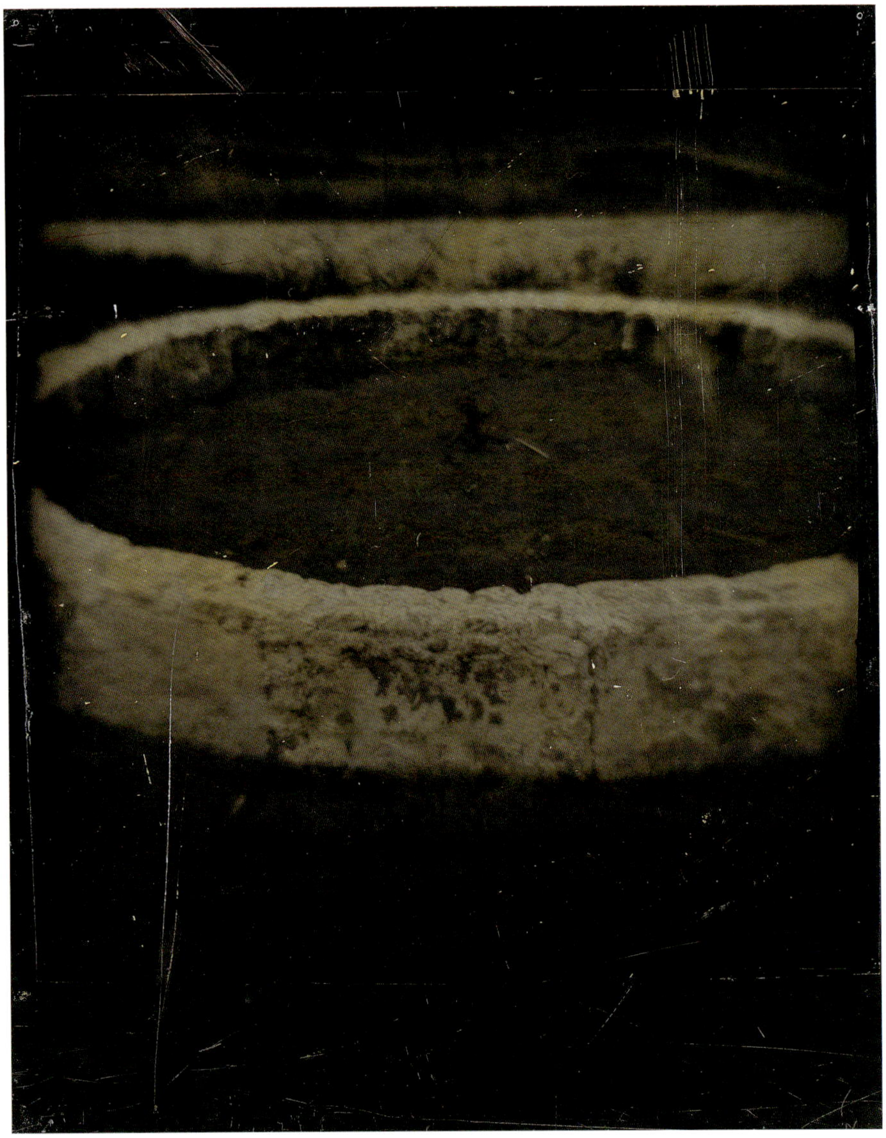

Plate 35
Untitled (Ring) 1990-91
Gelatin silver print with varnish and
scratches mounted on aluminum panel
60 x 48 in.
Collection of the artist

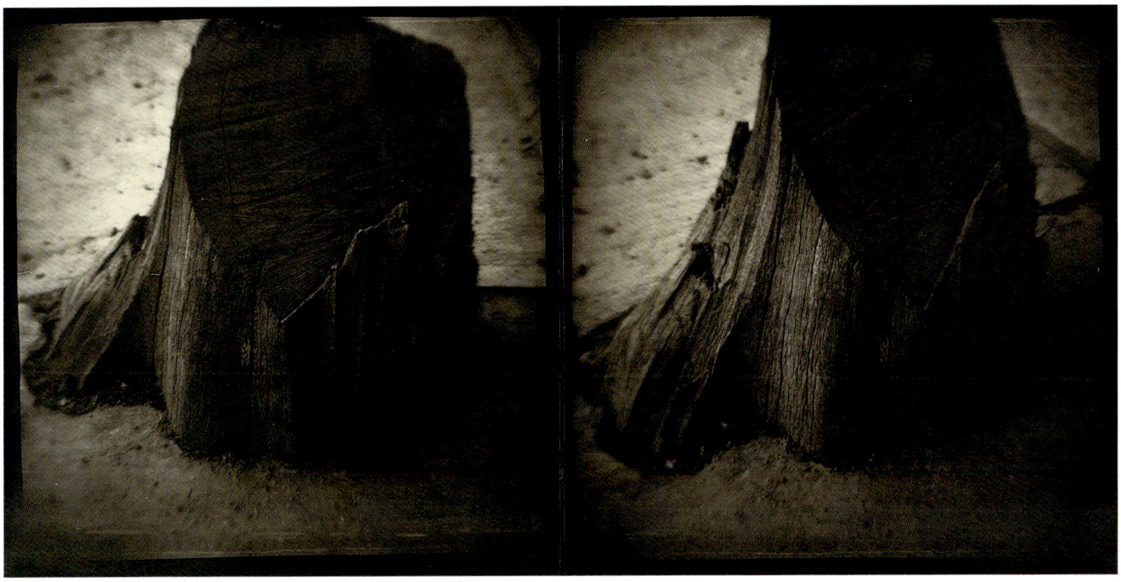

Panel 36
Untitled (Oaxaca stump) 1993
Gelatin silver prints mounted on wood panels
48 x 96 in.
Collection of the artist

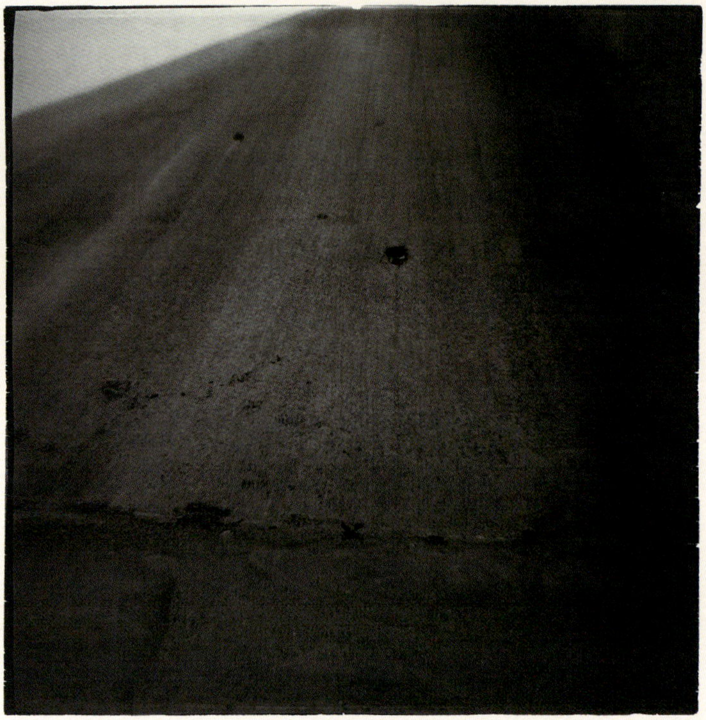

Plate 37
Untitled (Cone bank) 1995
Gelatin silver print mounted on wood panel
60 x 60 in.
Collection of the artist

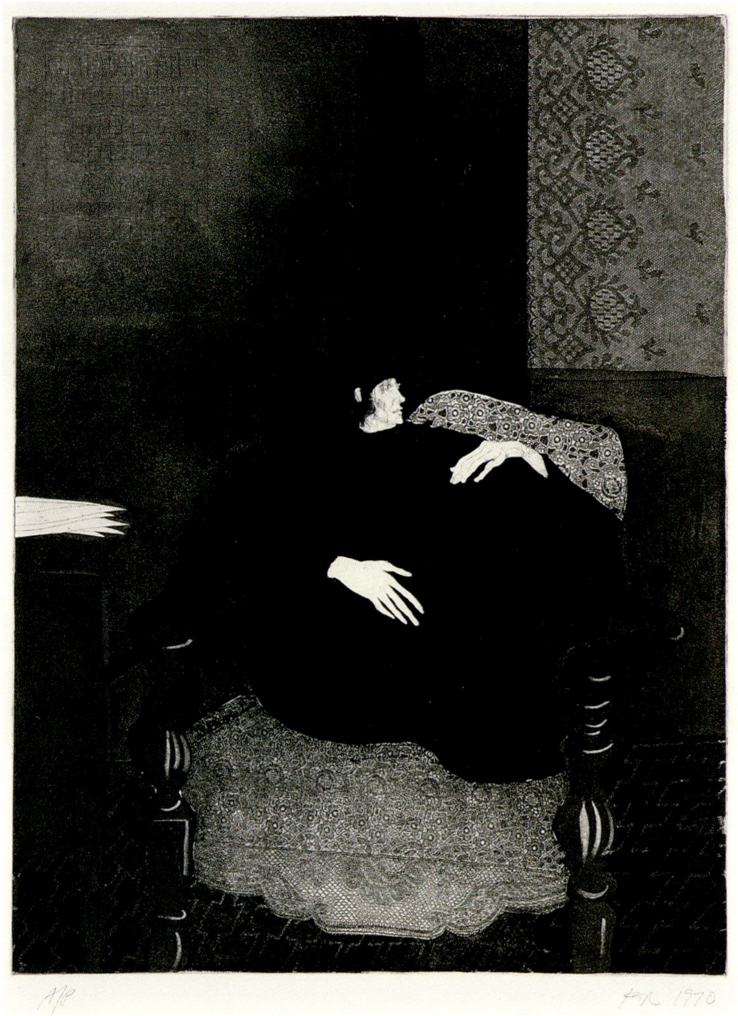

Plate 39
Untitled (Model in the Studio) 1970
Softground etching and aquatint
30 x 22 in.
Collection of the McNay Art Museum, Gift of the artist in memory of John Palmer Leeper

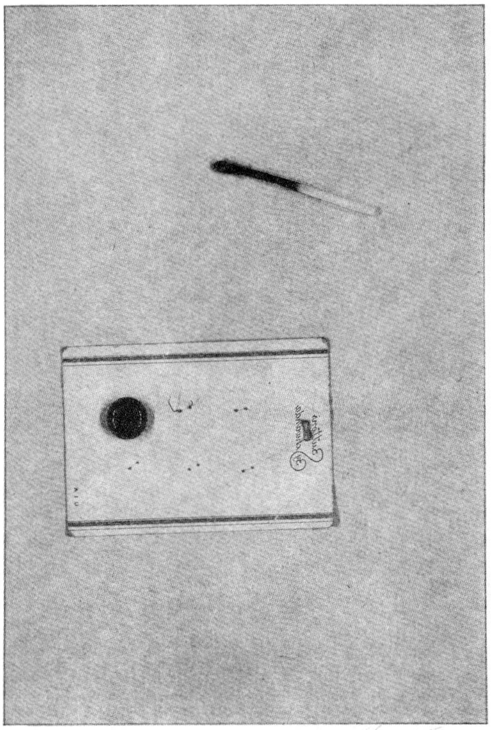

Plate 41
Untitled 1975
Photolithograph
16 1/2 x 13 in.
Collection of the McNay Art Museum, Gift of
the artist in memory of John Palmer Leeper

Plate 44
Untitled 1977
Lithograph
30 x 22 in.
Collection of the McNay Art Museum, Gift of
the artist in memory of John Palmer Leeper

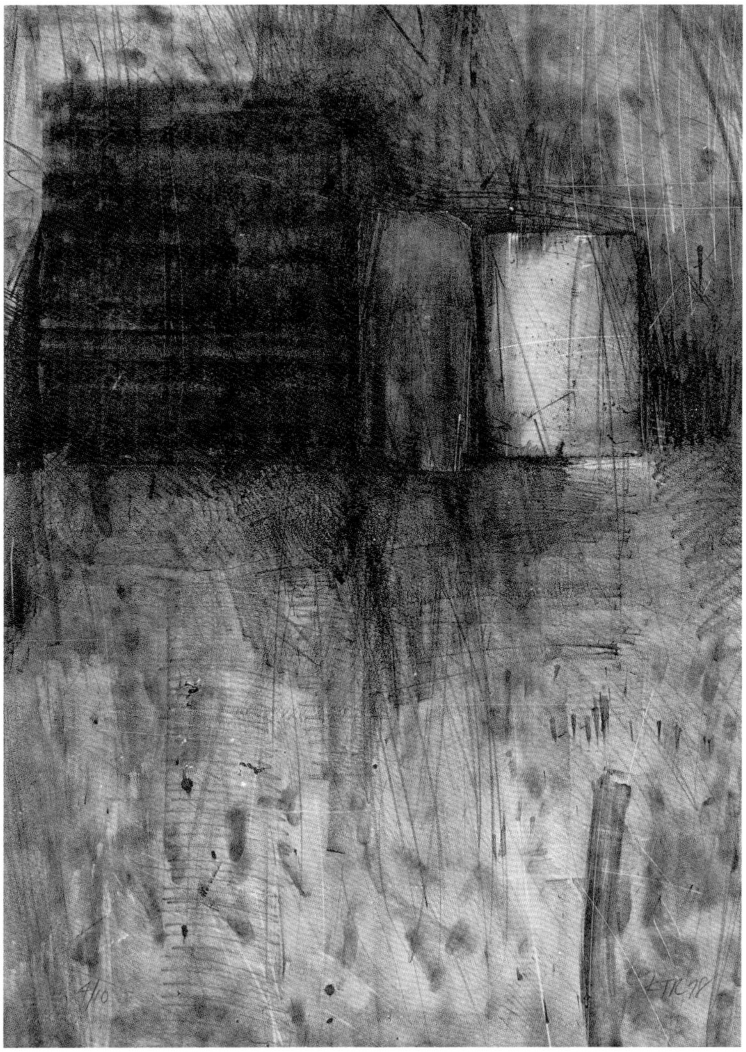

Plate 46
Untitled 1978
Lithograph
30 x 22 in.
Collection of the McNay Art Museum, Gift of
the artist in memory of John Palmer Leeper

Plate 49
Untitled (Maroon) 1983
Lithograph
22 1/2 x 27 3/4 in.
Collection of the McNay Art Museum, Gift of the artist in memory of John Palmer Leeper

Plate 53
Cant 1985
Lithograph
19 1/4 x 25 1/2 in.
Collection of the McNay Art Museum, Gift of
the artist in memory of John Palmer Leeper

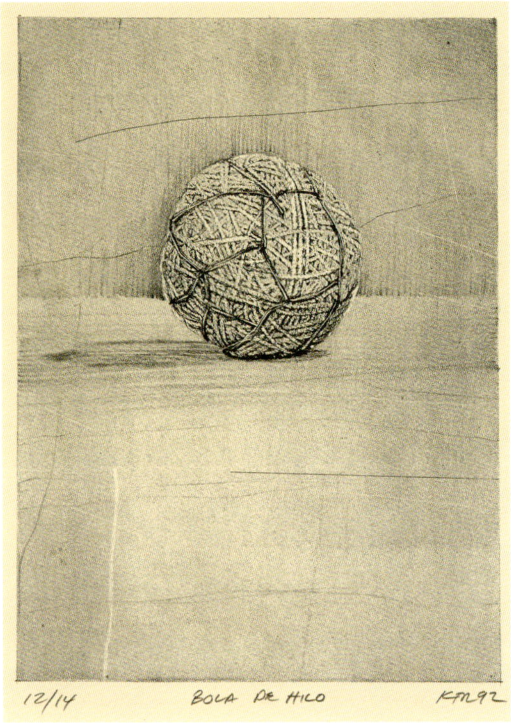

Plate 58
Bola de Hilo 1992
Lithograph
12 1/4 x 9 in.
Collection of the McNay Art Museum, Gift of
the artist in memory of John Palmer Leeper

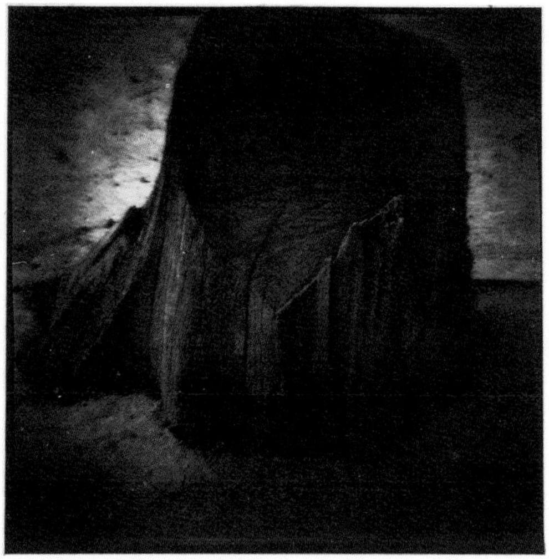

Plate 66
Untitled (Oaxaca stump) 1994
Collotype
14 x 11 in.
Collection of the McNay Art Museum, Gift of
the artist in memory of John Palmer Leeper

Chronology

1948	Born January 16, Hayward, California (San Francisco Bay Area) to Gwendolyn Gene and Melvin Wayne Rush. Third child after Wayne Albert and Melva Gwen
1954	Father dies. Mother begins elementary school teaching career to support family
1964	Studies art with Gerald Irving at Hayward High School, Hayward, California
1965-66	Studies art with Nikolaus Roukes at Hayward High School
1966-67	Studies architectural design and art at California State Polytechnic University, San Luis Obisbo, California
1967	Begins studies at California College of Arts and Crafts [CCAC], Oakland, California. Works for Hayward Area Recreation and Parks District in Plans and Designs Department surveying, mapmaking and illustrating
1968	Begins printmaking classes at CCAC, studies drawing and intaglio with Jeryl Parker
1969-70	Studies lithography with Robert Bechtle and Charles Gill at CCAC
1970	Receives B.F.A from California College of Arts and Crafts, Oakland, California
1970-72	Works for Hayward Area Recreation and Parks District, providing arts and crafts programs for handicapped clients at various institutions
1972-73	Moves to Raymond, New Hampshire. Works for Bradlees Department Stores in photographic, hardware, paint and seasonal departments
1973	Begins Graduate Printmaking Program at University of New Mexico [UNM], studying lithography under Garo Antreasian. Works as printer's assistant at Tamarind Institute of Lithography
1975	Receives M.A. from UNM
1976	First full time teaching appointment at San Antonio Art Institute [SAAI], San Antonio, Texas; starts printmaking program
1977	Receives first solo exhibition at Marion Koogler McNay Art Institute, exhibition curated by John Palmer Leeper

1979 Receives M.F.A. from University of Texas, Austin. Moves to Los Angeles, secures gallery, Art Space

1980 First Los Angeles-based show at Art Space, begins long-standing relationship with gallery director/owner, Lucy Adelman. Returns to San Francisco Bay Area in the fall to teach at CCAC for one year

1981 First exhibition at Bluxome Gallery, San Francisco, California

1982 Teaches lithography spring semester at San Francisco Art Institute. Returns to San Antonio in the fall to accept position as Assistant Professor of Art at the University of Texas at San Antonio [UTSA]

1986 With Richard Mogas, Jeffrey Moore, Adair Sutherland, Lewis Tarver and Richard Thompson, helps organize the Blue Star Exhibition and participates in founding of the Blue Star Art Space, San Antonio, Texas

1987 Technical treatise "Collotype: An Extension of Lithography" published in *Tamarind Papers*

1988 Receives Senior Fulbright Fellowship to teach printmaking courses at Taller de Las Artes Plásticas, "Rufino Tamayo," Oaxaca, México, fall semester. Becomes tenured professor at UTSA

1991 Marries artist, Haydeé Victoria Suescum, in San Antonio

1996 Kent Alejandro, born to Kent Rush and Haydeé Victoria Suescum in San Antonio, Texas

Private And Public Collections

Private Collections

Jonathan Abrams, Albuquerque, New Mexico

Lucy Adelman, Beverly Hills, California

Jesse Amado, San Antonio, Texas

Jeanne and Garo Antreasian, Albuquerque, New Mexico

Dana Asbury and Richard Levy, Albuquerque, New Mexico

Laurie and Thomas Barrow, Albuquerque, New Mexico

Gregg Bellow, Redwood City, California

Pam Berg, Los Angeles, California

Bonnie Bishop, Santa Fe, New Mexico

Diana Bontecou, Washington, D.C.

Sissie Burnside, San Antonio, Texas

Cindi and James Broderick, San Antonio, Texas

Sher Brooks and Robin Teague, San Antonio, Texas

Kitty Carlisle Hart, New York, New York

Rosie and Carlos Chavez, San Antonio, Texas

Pat Connolly, Orinda, California

Kim Corbin, San Antonio, Texas

Jean Davis, Los Angeles, California

Meredith Dean and Dennis Olsen, San Antonio, Texas

Michael Diaz, Santa Fe, New Mexico

Karen Doris and Damian Andrus, Albuquerque, New Mexico

Margaret Drewyer, Chicago, Illinois

Georgia and Chris Erck, San Antonio, Texas

Jefferson Erck, San Antonio, Texas

Sandra Field, Dallas, Texas

Janet Lennie Flohr and Bruce Flohr, San Antonio, Texas

Jack Ford, Oakland, California

Victoria Foster, Carmel, California

Claire S. Frankel, London, England

Paul Friedman, San Antonio, Texas

James Gandy, San Antonio, Texas

Melinda Gilbert, San Antonio, Texas

Elaine and Charles Gill, Oakland, California

Kathy and Ron Glowen, Seattle, Washington

A. Jose Gonzales, III, San Antonio, Texas

Michael Goodman, Beverly Hills, California

Lorraine and Charles Heasley, Cortland, New York

Bärbel Helmert, San Antonio, Texas

Margaret and Frank Johns, Napa, California

C. Bradley Justice, El Segundo, California

Pam and Wayne Kimball, Provo, Utah

Ellen Kirschman, Oakland, California

Ellie and Hal Lamb, San Antonio, Texas

Heather and Jerry Lammers, San Antonio, Texas

Terri Lane, San Antonio, Texas

Dan Lawrence, San Antonio, Texas

Marilyn and Leonard Lehrer, New York, New York

Kenneth Lerch, El Cerrito, California

Ann Livingston, San Antonio, Texas

Robert Lowe, Houston, Texas

Margo and Robert Marbut, San Antonio, Texas

Barbara Maulden, San Antonio, Texas

Ben Miller, Los Angeles, California

Richard Mogas, San Antonio, Texas

Janet Moses, Albuquerque, New Mexico

Jay Pinsky, Philadelphia, Pennsylvania

Elizabeth and Michael Powanda, Mill Valley, California

Anne Prince, San Antonio, Texas

Arden Reed, Claremont, California

Holly Roberts, Corrales, New Mexico

Diana Rodriguez Gil, San Antonio, Texas

Jack A. Rodgers, San Antonio, Texas

Gwendolyn Rush, Castro Valley, California

Noah Schafer and Thomas Prosser, La Verne, California

Miriam Scheffé, Berkeley, California

James Scott, Albuquerque, New Mexico

Robert Sennhauser, Houston, Texas

Michael A. Shiller, Albuquerque, New Mexico

Alice C. Simkins, San Antonio, Texas

Victoria and Jack Solovey, Corpus Christi, Texas

Aida and Alfredo Suescum, San Antonio, Texas

Hilje and Dirk Sybrandy, North Hollywood, California

Joan Tischler, San Antonio, Texas

Fernando Torres, Lima, Perú

Roger Travis, San Antonio, Texas

Bettie Ward, San Antonio, Texas

Margarita and Guillermo Urquiza, San Antonio, Texas

Anita and Mario Valencia, San Antonio, Texas

Colonel and Mrs. J.H. van Voorhis, Converse, Texas

Margaret Pace Willson and Robert Willson, San Antonio, Texas

Public Collections

Alamo Iron Works, San Antonio, Texas

Albuquerque Museum, Albuquerque, New Mexico

Angelo State University, San Angelo, Texas

Bartlett Cocke Inc., San Antonio, Texas

City of Dallas, Dallas, Texas

Eden United Church of Christ, Hayward, California

Instituto de Obra Gráfica de Oaxaca, Oaxaca, México

Marion Koogler McNay Art Museum, San Antonio, Texas

Matthews and Branscomb, San Antonio, Texas

Minot State College, Minot, North Dakota

Museu de Arte Contemporaneo Internacional, Salvador, Bahia, Brazíl

New Orleans Public Library, New Orleans, Louisiana

Oakland Museum, Oakland, California

Atkisson Gallery, Santa Barbara City College, Santa Barbara, California

Southeast Museum of Photography, Daytona Beach, Florida

Texas Arts Alliance, Austin, Texas

Elizabeth Coates Maddux Library, Trinity University, San Antonio, Texas

Tamarind Institute Archives, University Art Museum, University of New Mexico, Albuquerque, New Mexico

Humanities Research Center, University of Texas, Austin, Texas

United States Information Agency, Washington, D.C.

Selected Exhibitions

One-Person Exhibitions

1996 "Kent Rush," Milagros Gallery, San Antonio, Texas

1995 "Long Shots: Camera Images by Kent Rush," [ArtPace], San Antonio, Texas

1994 "Kent Rush: Photography," Martin Museum of Art, Baylor University, Waco, Texas

1993 "Kent Rush: Recent Photographs," Richard Levy Gallery, Albuquerque, New Mexico

1992 "Recent Works of Kent Rush," Dowd Fine Arts Center Gallery, State University of New York, Cortland, New York

1990 "Kent Rush: Recent Work," Coke Gallery, University of New Mexico Art Museum, Albuquerque

"Kent Rush: Grabados," Instituto Cultural Peruano Norteamericano, Lima, Perú

"Images: Photo Processes by Kent Rush," East Gallery, Texas Women's University Fine Arts Gallery, Denton, Texas

1989 "Kent Rush: Embankments," The Photographers Gallery, London, England

"Kent Rush: Forms and Attitudes," San Antonio Art League, San Antonio, Texas

1988 "Kent Rush: Embankments," Art Space, Los Angeles, California

"Obra Gráfica de Quince Años de Trabajo del Maestro Kent Rush," Galeria del Taller de las Artes Plásticas, "Rufino Tamayo," Oaxaca, México

1987 "Kent Rush: Embankment Series and Other Works," Koehler Cultural Center, San Antonio, Texas

1986 "Kent Rush: Paintings and Prints," Art Space, Los Angeles, California

1985 "Kent Rush: Drawings, Prints and Collages," University of Wisconsin Fine Arts Gallery, La Crosse, Wisconsin

1984 "Kent Rush: Paintings and Limited Edition Book, 'Snake'," Bluxome Gallery, San Francisco, California

1984 "Kent Rush: Snake," Marion Koogler McNay Art Museum, San Antonio, Texas

1982 "Kent Rush: Lithographs and Works on Paper," Department of Visual Arts Gallery, University of Wisconsin, Superior, Wisconsin

1979 "Kent Rush: Lithographs and Mixed-Media Paintings," Sol del Rio Gallery, San Antonio, Texas

1977 "Kent Rush: Works on Paper," Marion Koogler McNay Art Institute, San Antonio, Texas

1976 "Kent Rush: Lithography and Collage," Montalvo Center for the Arts, Saratoga, California

Selected Group Exhibitions

1997 New York Artist's Book and New Editions Fair, The Drawing Center, New York, New York

"Pop and Beyond: Contemporary Prints from the McNay Collection," Marion Koogler McNay Art Museum, San Antonio, Texas

1996 "Fresh Work," Southeast Museum of Photography, Daytona Beach, Florida

"Beyond Silver IV," Northlight Gallery and Image Dot Gallery, Arizona State University, Tempe, Arizona

"Darkness and Silence: The Photographic Works of Kate Breakey, Kent Rush and Kathy Vargas," Southwest Texas State University, San Marcos, Texas

1995 "Art Chicago '95," Richard Levy Gallery, Chicago, Illinois

"Blue Star on Houston Street," Dollar House, San Antonio, Texas

"Prints," Richard Levy Gallery, Albuquerque, New Mexico

"Cliché-verre," Arkansas State University Art Gallery, Jonesboro, Arkansas

"Prints: Recent Works," The Artists' Gallery, San Antonio, Texas

1994 "Drawing/Crossing the Line," Diverse Works, Houston, Texas

"Compelling Spaces," Laguna Gloria Art Museum, Austin, Texas

"American Photography: A History in Pictures," San Antonio Museum of Art, San Antonio, Texas

"Texas Dialogues: Houston/San Antonio," Blue Star Art Space, San Antonio, Texas

"Putting it on Paper: Contemporary Graphics by San Antonio Artists," Marion Koogler McNay Art Museum, San Antonio, Texas

1993 "Matrix I: Kate Petley/Kent Rush," Art Museum of South Texas, Corpus Christi, Texas

"Crossing Territories," Santa Fe Museum of Fine Arts, Santa Fe, New Mexico

"Social Studies/Public Monuments," The Center for Photography at Woodstock, New York and The Ulrich Museum of Art, Wichita, Kansas

"The Everpresent Moment: Contemporary Drawings," The Selby Gallery, Ringling School of Art and Design, Sarasota, Florida

1992 "Contemporary Texas Printmakers," Emison Art Center, DePauw University, Greencastle, Indiana

"On Photography," Arlington, Museum of Art, Arlington, Texas

"1991 Mid-American Arts Alliance Award Winning Photographers," Art St. Louis, St. Louis, Missouri

1991 "12th University of Dallas Print Invitational," University of Dallas, Irving, Texas

Richard Levy Gallery, Albuquerque, New Mexico

1990 "Texas Dialogues: Austin/San Antonio," Blue Star Art Space, San Antonio, Texas

"Fundamentals of Photography: A Survey of Photographic Processes," University Art Museum, University of New Mexico, Albuquerque, New Mexico

1990 "Ellis Island Project," Montclair Art Museum, Montclair, New Jersey

"9th Biennial Drake Print Symposium Exhibition," Harmon Fine Arts Center, Drake University, Des Moines, Iowa

1989 Universidad Nacional Autónoma de México Extención, San Antonio, Texas

"Wayne Kimball, Dennis Olsen and Kent Rush: Printmaking Invitational," University Gallery, Baylor University, Waco, Texas

"Texas Printmaking '89 Invitational," Mexicarte Art Museum, Austin, Texas

1988 "Forms and Attitudes: Kent Rush and Louis Turner," San Antonio Art Institute, San Antonio, Texas

"Texas: Exploring the Boundaries (FOTOFEST' 88)," Lawndale Art and Performance Center, Houston, Texas

"McNay and Texas Artists," Marion Koogler McNay Art Museum, San Antonio, Texas

1987 "Texas Annual 1987," Laguna Gloria Art Museum, Austin, Texas

"Florence Prints: Works from Santa Reparata," St. Mary's College, Notre Dame University, South Bend, Indiana

1986 "Introductions '86," Adams/Middleton Gallery, Dallas, Texas

"The Blue Star Exhibition," Blue Star Art Space, San Antonio, Texas

"Papel Arte," Museu de Arte Contemporánea Internacional, Salvador, Bahia, Brazíl

"SAMA OPEN '86," San Antonio Museum of Art, San Antonio, Texas

"Recent Photography," Blue Collar Gallery, San Antonio, Texas

1985 "Paperworks," Marion Koogler McNay Art Museum, San Antonio, Texas

"Discoveries II," Lawndale Art and Performance Center, Houston, Texas

"The Philadelphia Print Club: 61st International Competition," Philadelphia, Pennsylvania

"Cameron National Print Exhibition," University Art Gallery, Cameron University, Lawton, Oklahoma

1984 "Washington and Jefferson National Painting Show," Washington and Jefferson College, Washington, Pennsylvania

"Across Texas," Patrick Graphics Gallery, Austin, Texas

"Printmakers," Charlton Art Gallery, San Antonio, Texas

1983 "Prints from the California College of Arts and Crafts," World Print Council Gallery, Fort Mason, San Francisco, California

"6th Hawaii National Print Exhibition," Honolulu Academy of Arts, Honolulu, Hawaii

1982 "Introducing Richard Putz, Sculpture and Kent Rush, Etchings and Paintings," Bluxome Gallery, San Francisco, California

"Seventh British International Print Biennale," Bradford Art Galleries, Bradford, England

1981 "Kent Rush and Douglas Meyer," Art Space, Los Angeles, California

"Approaches to Reality: Lithographs by Bay Area Artists," Kaiser Center Art Gallery, Oakland, California

"Premier Exhibition," McKonkey/Foster Gallery, San Antonio, Texas

1980 "Cliché-verre: Hand Drawn, Light Printed," Detroit Institute of the Arts, Detroit, Michigan and also Museum of Fine Arts, Houston, Texas

"Opening Exhibition," Objects Gallery, San Antonio, Texas

1979 "Paperworks: An Exhibition of Texas Artists," Witte Museum, San Antonio, Texas

1978 "Wanted: Texas Art," University Union Gallery, California State Polytechnic University, Pomona, California

"National Exhibition of Works on or of Paper and Clay," Memphis State University Art Gallery, Memphis, Tennessee

1977 "Works on paper by Contemporary American Artists," Madison Art Center, Madison, Wisconsin

"L.A. Printmaking Society 5th National Exhibition," University California at Northridge, California

1976 "2nd Annual Regional Invitational," Koehler Cultural Center, San Antonio, Texas

1975 "1975 New Mexico Fine Arts Biennial," Museum of New Mexico, Santa Fe, New Mexico

1974 "Exposure '74," University of Northern Illinois, Dekalb, Illinois

1973 "Contemporary Prints from American Universities," (United States Information Agency), Aman, Jordan; Bankok, Thailand; Buenos Aires, Argentina; Islamabad, Pakistan; Kinshasa, Zaire; Lima, Perú; Lisbon, Portugal; Manila, Phillipines; Ottawa, Canada; Santiago, Chile; La Paz, Bolivia

1972 "3rd Annual Regional Art Competition," San Jose Museum of Art, San Jose, California

1971 "Phelan Awards: Photography 1971," Oakland Museum of Art, Oakland, California

1970 "Young Printmakers 1970," Indianapolis Museum of Art, Indianapolis, Indiana

Bibliography

Catalogues

Bradley, Steven. "The Blue Star Exhibition," Blue Star Contemporary Art Space, San Antonio, Texas, 1986

Brunon, Bernard. "Drawing/Crossing the Line," Diverse Works, Houston, Texas, 1994

Gaston, Diana. "Kent Rush: Recent Works," Fine Arts Museum, University of New Mexico, Albuquerque, New Mexico, 1990

Glowen, Ron. "Kent Rush: Forms and Attitudes," San Antonio Art League, San Antonio, Texas, 1989

Heasley, Charles. "Recent Works of Kent Rush," Dowd Fine Arts Gallery, State University of New York, Cortland, New York, 1992

Leeper, John Palmer. "Works on Paper-Kent Rush," Marion Koogler McNay Art Museum, San Antonio, Texas, 1977

Mason, Wally. "The Everpresent Moment: Contemporary Drawing," Selby Gallery, Ringling School of Art, Sarasota, Florida, 1993

Miller, Laurence. "Texas Dialogues: Austin - San Antonio," Blue Star Art Space, San Antonio, Texas, December 1991

Smith, Mark Lesley. "Reflections on the Art-Life Continuum," Texas Fine Arts Association, Austin, Texas, 1995

Symmes, Marilyn. "Cliché-verre in the 20th Century," Detroit Institute of the Arts, Detroit, Michigan, 1980

Periodicals and Books

Armitage, Diane. "Kent Rush: Recent Photographs," *The Magazine,* December 1993, Volume 2, Number 6, pg.65

Bennett, Steve. "Artist of the Year: Local painter receives honor for artistic vision in photographs," *San Antonio Light,* January 14, 1990, pg. K-1

Boswell, Peter. "Urban Imagery," *Artweek,* July 31, 1982, pg.5

Brunner, Kath & Riedel, Eric. "Discoveries II," *The Lawndale Inquirer,* December 1985, pg.24

Castro, Fernando. "Ken Rush y sus técnicas de grabado," Lima, *El Comercio,* October 21, 1990, pg. C2

Gardener, Colin. "The Galleries: West Los Angeles," *Los Angeles Times,* April 4, 1986, Section IV, pg.V9-11

Goddard, Dan. "Dreamscapes & Realities: Milagros Celebrates The Contrasting Visions of Two Artists," *San Antonio Express-News,* November 25, 1996, pg. D1, 3

Goddard, Dan. "S.A., El Paso Get Together For A 'Dialogue' About Art: A Tale of Two Cities on Exhibit at Blue Star," *San Antonio Express-News,* January 21, 1990, pg. H1

Greenberg, Mike. "Where The Art Is," *San Antonio Express-News,* October 4, 1981, pg. M5

Hammond, Pamela. "Kent Rush at Art Space," *Images and Issues,* Spring, 1982, pg. 87

Hemmerdinger, William. "Towards the Finish Line," *Artweek,* May 1980, pg. 6

King, Marcia. "New Art Energy in S.A.," *San Antonio Express-News*, December 2, 1976, pg. D10

Leeper, John Palmer. "Two Exhibitions Refreshing San Antonio," *North San Antonio Times*, August 16, 1979, pg. 5

Markette, Karen. "'Snake' - Blending Poetry, The Abstract," San Antonio *Revue*, April, 1984, pg. 5

Muchnic, Suzanne. "The Galleries: West Los Angeles," *Los Angeles Times*, April 18, 1980, Section VI, pg. 10

Pincus, R.L. "The Galleries: West Los Angeles," *Los Angeles Times*, October 7, 1983, Part VI pg. 13

Rutledge, Virginia. "Social Studies/Public Monuments: Partial Documents: Contemporary Photography on the Street," *Photography Center Quarterly* #55, Spring 1993

Solon, Marcia Goren. "Work of Artist Kent Rush Makes Concrete Abstract," *San Antonio Light*, February 8, 1987, Section J, pg. 2

Symmes, Marilyn. "Clichés-verres: Prints Made Without Ink or Press," San Francisco, *Print News*, April/May, 1990, pg. 3

Valencia, Anita. "Medium Inspires Artists," San Antonio, *The Paisano*, November 6, 1984, pg. 5

Weser, Marcia Goren. "Current Show At Institute Has Artfully Matched Works," *San Antonio Light*, July 3, 1988, pg. N3

Glossary

ACRYLIC—a plastic-based liquid used as an alternative to oil as a medium for painting. Its main advantage is that it dries much more quickly than oil-based pigments. (see casein)

AQUATINT—a printmaking process similar to etching. In the process, a metal plate is dusted with an acid-resisting substance, usually a rosin. This substance does not cover the plate completely, so it does not resist the acid completely. The copper beneath each speck of rosin is protected but the copper between the specks gets bitten by the acid. When these bitten areas are inked, printed, and magnified they appear as lines encircling islands of white. The process is used because it can produce areas of tone. It is called aquatint because these tones often have the appearance of watercolor washes. (see catalogue 39)

CASEIN—a milk-based liquid in which pigments can be suspended for painting. Areas which have been painted with casein have a very flat, matte finish. (see catalogue 24; see also acrylic)

CHINE-COLLÉ—a French term literally translated as "glued china," china referring to a type of thin, colored tissue paper. The term describes the application of a different sheet of paper during the printing process that adds color and texture to the print. Usually, the chine-collé paper is glued to the primary paper support, then put through the printing press. The image is then printed on top of the added sheet. (see catalogue 55)

COLLAGE—a term derived from the French word *coller* which means to glue, paste, or stick-together. In art it refers to works of art on paper in which two or more different elements are combined to form a single composition.

COLLOTYPE—a printmaking process in which a light-sensitive gel is exposed using a photographic negative. When the gel is exposed to the light it hardens creating a very fine pattern of reticulated lines. The exposed, or hardened, parts of the gel then receive the printer's ink and are printed onto a piece of paper. The resulting image has, over its surface, a fine pattern of lines which when magnified has the appearance of dry, cracked earth. This pattern of lines usually imparts a soft, overall tone to the final image. (see catalogue 66; see also aquatint)

CYANOTYPE—an early and simple photographic process which utilizes iron salts exposed to light to create an image which can be printed directly on paper. Invented in 1842, it is commonly used to make blueprints. (see catalogue 28)

ETCHING—a printmaking process, developed in the sixteenth century, in which a metal plate, usually copper, is coated with an acid-resisting substance called a ground. The artist scratches, with an etching needle, his design into this ground, exposing the copper beneath. The whole plate is dipped into an acid bath. The acid bites into the exposed copper, creating incised lines. These lines are then filled with ink and the plate printed. (see catalogue 39)

GELATIN SILVER PRINT—a photographic process in which light-sensitive silver bromide is suspended in a gelatin emulsion. The process, introduced in the 1880s, has been most popular with artists because of its great tonal range. (see catalogue 31)

LITHOGRAPHY—a printmaking method, based on the fact that oil and water do not mix, developed in the early nineteenth century. In the process, the artist draws his design onto the surface of a piece of limestone using a greasy ink specially developed for lithography. The design is fixed to the stone with a mixture of water and very weak acid. When the stone is printed, the greasy printing ink is attracted to the artist's design but repelled by those areas of stone covered with water. A sheet of paper is then laid on top of the stone and the image is printed on it. The medium has long been a favorite of artists because of its ability to transfer directly drawings to a printed form and because of its ability to produce a wide range of lines and tones. (see catalogue 44) In a color lithograph, the color is usually applied with a separate stone. (see catalogue 49)

PHOTOGRAVURE—a printmaking process which combines etching and photography. Rather than manually create a design with an etching needle, the artist transfers his design with a photographic transparency onto a copper plate that has been coated with a light-sensitive, acid-resisting ground. The transferred design is then etched and inked. In the nineteenth century, the process was used to make high-quality reproductions of paintings and drawings. Many contemporary artists, however, have used the medium to create original works of art. (see catalogue 68)

PHOTOLITHOGRAPHY—a printmaking process which combines lithography and photography. Rather than draw directly onto a lithographic stone or plate, the artist transfers his design photochemically onto a surface which has been sensitized to light. (see catalogue 41)

WOODCUT—the earliest and simplest printmaking technique. The earliest woodcuts known were created in the fourteenth century. In the process, the artist carves his design into a block of wood leaving in relief those areas he wants to print and carving away those areas he does not. The areas left in relief are inked and printed. (see catalogue 48)

Distributed by The University of Texas Press

ISBN: 0-916677-40-0

Library of Congress Catalog Card Number: 98-66836

Editors: Allison Hays Lane
Susan Kaufman
Roslyn E. B. Walker

Designer: DeLinda Stephens, Command P

Photography: Michael Jay Smith
[Frontispiece] Lyle W. Williams

Color Separation and Production: Command P